A RESOURCE BOOK FOR ESL/EFL TEACHERS

PROVOKING THOUGHT

Memory and Thinking in ELT

HALL HOUSTON

Anthimeria Press

ISBN: 1-4392-5199-1
ISBN-13: 9781439251997

Visit www.booksurge.com to order additional copies.

ACKNOWLEDGEMENTS

I would like to thank the following teachers whose wise comments greatly improved the contents of this book:

Mark Brooke
Daya Datwani Choy
Matthew Hunter
Drew McEwan
Monique Roques
Andrew Starck

Special thanks to Adam Khan, Chic Thompson, Vincent Ryan Ruggiero and Julie Plenty who granted me permission to include their superb articles and book excerpts here. Also, thanks to Marilee Sprenger, Alane Starko, and Vincent Ryan Ruggiero for participating in the interviews.

And this book is dedicated to my family, who are always in my thoughts.

TABLE OF CONTENTS

INTRODUCTION

"Learning without thought is labor lost." - Confucius

This book, *Provoking Thought,* is a resource book of activities for the language classroom. The activities are designed for an ESL/EFL context, but they can also be adapted for teaching other languages. The five chapters here cover five areas: thinking, memory, creativity, critical thinking, and expressing thought in writing. These areas can enhance language learning, impelling students to develop greater fluency. This book is ideal for teachers who want to help students improve their English as well as develop thinking skills that can be useful in everyday life.

THINKING

Psychologists and philosophers have puzzled over the nature of thinking for centuries. Just what is thinking?

- Thinking is an individual process. In order to think, one must detach from the outside world and start putting thoughts together. Everyone has a different thinking style and different preferences.

- Thinking is invisible. We cannot see what our students are thinking. Likewise, they cannot see what we are thinking. We can only make guesses based on facial expressions, gestures, and posture. However, thought can be expressed through language and other forms.

- Thinking can have a serious impact on our lives. Optimistic thinking and visualization can give us strength, whereas negative thoughts can drag us down.

- Thinking can allow us to do things that are quite impossible in real life. We can fantasize, revisit the past, make elaborate plans, or even think about nothing.

Our students' thoughts are a valuable resource in the classroom. When students take a moment to gather their thoughts about an idea or a topic, then express themselves in English, they can become more fluent, as they learn to say things they never said before.

THINKING SKILLS

Benjamin Bloom's taxonomy of thinking skills is a frequently cited resource for the teaching of thinking skills. He differentiates between lower level and higher level thinking skills.

Bloom mentions three categories of lower level thinking skills: knowledge, comprehension, and application. At the knowledge level, students remember information. At the comprehension level, students put information into their own words. At the application level, students apply information to new contexts.

The three categories of higher level thinking skills are analysis, synthesis, and evaluation. At the analysis level, students break up information into parts. At the synthesis level, students take information and produce a new pattern. At the evaluation level, students judge information based on their own criteria.

Recently, Lorin Anderson and David Krathwohl, working together with experts in such fields as cognitive psychology and curriculum and instruction, have produced an updated version of Bloom's taxonomy. Here are the six revised categories:

Remembering: Retrieving, recognizing, and recalling relevant knowledge from long-term memory.

Understanding: Constructing meaning from oral, written, and graphic messages through interpreting, exemplifying, classifying, summarizing, inferring, comparing, and explaining.

Applying: Carrying out or using a procedure through executing, or implementing.

Analyzing: Breaking material into constituent parts, determining how the parts relate to one another and to an overall structure or purpose through differentiating, organizing, and attributing.

Evaluating: Making judgments based on criteria and standards through checking and critiquing.

Creating: Putting elements together to form a coherent or functional whole; reorganizing elements into a new pattern or structure through generating, planning, or producing.

(source: Anderson & Krathwohl, 2001, pp. 67-68)

Let's examine how a teacher might use an article about a historical event to develop these six skills.

Remembering – students recall names or dates mentioned in the article.
Understanding – students relay the major points of the event.
Applying – students develop a theory of why the event occurred.
Analyzing – students isolate the different parts of the event.
Evaluating – students judge the decisions made by leaders during this event.
Creating – students write essays from the point of view of an eyewitness.

As you plan your lessons, you can consider how to help students develop these skills. This book addresses these skills, but in the context of language learning. While many exercises in this book can support thinking skills, the emphasis is on using thinking as a resource and a springboard for fluency practice.

AIMS OF THIS BOOK

One aim of this book is to create a learner-centered atmosphere. These activities encourage students to share their thoughts, feelings, ideas, and opinions. This can make learning English more personalized and therefore more motivating than following a coursebook written for a mass audience which may not appeal to your students. However, many activities in this book can be used in combination with a coursebook.

Another aim is to emphasize real topics and ideas, not grammatical structures and sentence patterns. The activities contained in this book will take students away from rote learning towards meaningful learning which can help increase the rate at which students improve.

Still another aim is to help develop academic skills. You can use some of the activities in this book to help students produce their own ideas, create sound arguments for a position, participate in debates and discussions, and write academic papers.

TEACHING TIPS

Here are some general guidelines for using thinking as a resource:

Choose compelling topics. If you expect students to spend a lot of time working on a topic, aim for one they will be interested in. Controversial topics are ideal, as there is more room for discussion when students disagree. You can also choose topics that relate to current events in the area where you teach. Your colleagues and students can provide some useful suggestions.

Teach students how to do research. Show students how to find out more information about a topic. Students have more to say about a subject when they have a deeper understanding of it.

Provide thinking time. Don't expect students to come up with ideas immediately. Routinely allow a few minutes for them gather their thoughts.

Praise students' attempts to express their ideas. If you are dealing with a class that is not accustomed to giving their opinions in class, support them and encourage them to verbalize their thoughts.

Provide a range of stimuli to provoke more thought. You can use pictures, poems, songs, instrumental music, texts, quotes, and even sound effects to keep their thinking fresh.

Demonstrate useful language for different activities. Suggest phrases students can use to offer ideas and share criticism. For example, during a brainstorming activity, you can provide sentence starters such as "How about...?" or "I'd like to suggest..."

ERROR CORRECTION

In most of the activities contained in this book, the emphasis is on fluency not accuracy. However, we needn't ignore error correction. While there is much disagreement about the positive effects of correction, I think it's important for two reasons to point out errors: students often expect it, and it can have some influence on avoiding fossilization of errors.

It's wise to use a variety of correction techniques, including:

* on the spot verbal correction
* writing a correct version on the board

* setting aside time in class to discuss errors you overheard
* giving students each a note mentioning one or two errors
* pointing out what they got right as well as their errors
* reformulation (restating a student's utterance with errors corrected)
* asking a student to restate his sentence without saying where the error is
* encouraging students to correct each other

Due to class size or other constraints, you might not be able to in-corporate all of these techniques into your teaching. Consider also the option of not correcting errors. An excess of error correction can be discouraging for students. Nevertheless, some use of error correc-tion can help students see where they need to improve. It also shows them that you do pay attention to their errors!

FOCUS ON FORM

Focus on form activities can also help students develop accuracy as well as fluency. Focus on form activities are often used as part of task-based lessons, where students are encouraged to notice certain lan-guage features. In listening and reading activities, students should be encouraged to make note of new language. Ask them to highlight new words and phrases, and write down new expressions they hear. Also, teachers can take additional steps to point out structures. For example, if you give students an article that contains several uses of the passive voice, you can ask students to underline them or write them up on the board. You can assign students to jot down some of the new language they encounter. From time to time, you can ask stu-dents to review their notes. (For more about focus on form activities in a task-based lesson, read Chapter Six of *Doing Task-Based Teaching* by Dave Willis and Jane Willis. Also, Luke Meddings and Scott Thornbury have some intriguing focus on form activities based on the Dogme approach in their book *Teaching Unplugged*.)

Tips for using the activities in this book with your classes:

1. Use the activities sparingly. Don't try to use them all at once. Find one or two that you think might be effective, then test them out.

2. Look for ways to integrate the activities into your lessons. Some activities might work well as warmers, while others might be good for getting students to expand on some of the topics you have discussed in class. A few activities in Chapter One, such as Thought of the day, Lateral thinking puzzles, and Riddles (activities 1.4 to 1.6), might become a popular thread, an activity that becomes a regular feature of a class.

3. Feel free to adapt the activities as you wish. Some of the writing activities can be transformed into speaking activities. You might find that an activity works better in an abbreviated form, or think of an ingenious way to expand on it.

4. Some activities may fulfill more than one purpose. For example, Activity 2.4, How We Learn New Words can be found in the chapter on memory, but it's also a brainstorming activity.

5. Pay close attention to the layout of your classroom. Experiment with different seating arrangements. You can put chairs in a circle, a semi-circle, small circles of 3 or 4, or lines of seats facing each other.

OVERVIEW OF CHAPTERS

Here's a summary of what you will find in this book:

Chapter One, Thinking, covers the topic of thinking. It includes activities such as lateral thinking puzzles and riddles, which involve asking students to speculate and guess. Other activities focus on our everyday thinking patterns. Use activities from this chapter as a starting point for activities from other chapters in this book.

Chapter Two, Memory, is about how we learn and remember. While memory is not thought of as a skill in the way that creative thinking and critical thinking are, several memory techniques, such as the story method, can be extremely beneficial in helping students consolidate what they've learned. This chapter contains numerous practical suggestions for helping students remember new language and review vocabulary from previous lessons. Using the activities in this chapter, students also will learn some effective ways to remember names, talk about their own memories and discuss some common memory problems.

Chapter Three, Creativity, emphasizes motivating students to generate new and interesting thoughts. Creativity is a skill that writers, advertisers, artists, businesspeople and musicians strive to develop. In order to be creative, it's important to suspend judgment and be open to looking at things from new perspectives. With the activities in this chapter, students can develop their creativity through idea generation and problem solving. You might use these activities for fluency practice or as a way to help students come up with ideas for a project or writing assignment.

Chapter Four, Critical Thinking, is about getting students to judge their own ideas, as well as the ideas of others. Critical thinking courses teach valuable skills including how to structure an argument, how to find support for your arguments, and how to spot logical fallacies. Using the activities in this chapter, students can learn how to develop their critical thinking skills as they read news articles and advertisements. In addition, they can learn to examine arguments skillfully.

Chapter Five, Organizing Ideas on Paper, contains a variety of ways for students to express their thoughts in writing. These include graphic organizers, which are useful in reading classes. The chapter also contains some creative projects and ways of getting feedback from students.

Another feature of this book is a series of interviews with experts on memory, creativity, and critical thinking. These interviews show how these three topics intersect with education and share expert information on these subjects for teachers who would like to learn more.

At the back of the book, you will find an index where you can see activities organized according to type. This can save time when looking for a particular type of activity to use in class.

I would be interested in hearing about how these activities worked out in your classroom. Please contact me at **hallhouston@yahoo.com** if you have any comments about this book. Also, visit my website for more teaching ideas:

www.hallhouston.com

1
Thinking

This first chapter addresses the topic of thinking. Thinking is an essential part of every class, yet it is often overlooked. The activities contained in this first chapter open up the topic of thinking and our everyday thinking habits. There are a number of activities that can be used as warmers, such as riddles and lateral thinking puzzles. In addition, there is a wide range of activities that focus on the nature of thinking. Use the activities here to make students aware of their own thought processes or to encourage reflection. First we will look at some different thinking styles, along with reflective teaching.

THINKING STYLES

Allen Harrison and Robert Bramson describe five major thinking styles in their book *The Art of Thinking*. These six styles are:

The Synthesist – creative and speculative, likes to make new combinations of things
The Idealist – focuses on the future, looks for the perfect solution
The Pragmatist – wants to get things done, looks for the quickest solution
The Analyst – believes in following methods and formulas, wants a scientific solution
The Realist – relies on what he sees and hears to evaluate, wants to know the facts

Let's examine how these five thinking styles might influence a teacher's lesson planning. A synthesist might imagine how an unusual combination of activities (a role play mixed with a dictation) might make for a fruitful learning experience. An idealist might design lessons with particular aims in mind. A pragmatist might want to use a lesson plan that's worked successfully many times before. An analyst might base every lesson on the latest second language acquisition research. Finally, a realist might construct lesson plans that reflect what he or she has seen and heard in the classroom over many years of teaching.

These differing approaches to lesson planning all stem from different thinking styles. None is superior to the others. After reading this, you might find you easily identify with one of these types. However, you might consider adopting one of the other thinking styles to gain more perspective on your teaching.

REFLECTIVE TEACHING

Reflective teaching refers to the process of thinking about your teaching, analyzing what you do, and considering other possibilities. It emphasizes clarifying the reasons behind every step you take in the classroom.

You can start with simply taking notes after a lesson. You can write about something that went well or a situation you hope to change. For example, you might write about a conflict you are having with a student or a group of students, then document the steps you take to ameliorate the situation.

A more ambitious form of taking notes is keeping a teacher diary. You can spend a few minutes after each lesson taking notes on what you experienced in class.

However, reflective teaching need not be a solitary process. You can integrate your own thoughts with a peer observation from another teacher. Another idea is to provide opportunities for feedback from your students. Chapter Five of this book has several activities for getting student feedback. (<u>Reflective Teaching in Second Language Classrooms</u> by Jack C. Richards and Charles Lockhart is a recommended resource on reflective teaching. See Duncan Foord's <u>The Developing Teacher</u> for more information on keeping a teacher diary, as well as other suggestions for professional development.)

———

1.1 Random thoughts

Aims – Writing, vocabulary, speaking
Time - 20 minutes
Preparation – None

1. Write the word *think* in the middle of the board.

2. Tell students to write whatever words and phrases they associate with the word in the area around it. Suggest they draw arrows from *think* to the words and phrases they write.

3. Encourage students to continue the associations with the words they just wrote. Tell them to add drawings if they wish.

4. After a few minutes, tell them to stop and look over their work. Invite students to speculate on some of the associations, and ask each other about what they wrote.

5. Next ask students to return to their desks. Tell each student to write 5 A's and B's (A B A B A B A B A B), vertically on the left side of the page. Ask them to write one word from the previous part of the exercise on each line, either in the beginning, middle or end of the line. They should leave the rest of each line blank.

6. Now students should exchange papers with a partner. Each student must write out a conversation between two people (A and B), with each line incorporating the word their partner wrote down.

7. Put students into pairs, and ask them to choose one of the conversations to present to the class. Invite several pairs to perform their conversations for the class.

Variation: If possible, you can do steps 1-4 on the floor or another flat surface that can be written on with chalk.

1.2 Thinking about collocations and chunks

Aims – Learning collocations and chunks, making sentences
Time - 20 minutes
Preparation – None

1. Write the word *think* on the board.

2. Put students into pairs. Ask them to make a list of all the different forms of think (thought, thinker, etc.) In addition, get the pairs to think of two words that mean think and two words that mean the opposite.

3. Ask several pairs to call out their words.

4. Now dictate the following list of phrases to the class:

think tank
a penny for your thoughts
think for yourself
think fast
thinking of you
think again
groupthink
come to think of it
second thoughts
wishful thinking
put on your thinking cap
food for thought

5. Have one student write the list on the board. Check for errors, and ask students if they understand the phrases. Explain the phrases they don't know and give examples. Encourage students to contribute any additional phrases they know using the word think.

6. Now have students all come to the board and write down any phrases using think/thinking/thought from their first languages, and add English translations.

7. Put students into pairs, and ask them to write a short sentence using one of the English phrases from the list in step 4 and write it at the bottom of a sheet of paper. Then they should draw a picture that illustrates the phrase.

8. Put all the pictures up on the board for the class to look over.

Variation: Use a different word for this exercise, perhaps one that relates to the topic of your lesson.

1.3 Train of thought

Aims – Forming questions, guessing
Time - 5-10 minutes
Preparation - Take note of your thoughts on the way to school and right before class.

1. When class begins, invite students to speculate on the progression of your thoughts in the hours before class. Call on several students to guess what you were thinking about. Take notes of their comments on the board.

2. Tell them which answers were right and which were wrong.

Extension: You can have students repeat the activity in pairs.

1.4 Thought of the day

Aims – Reading, sharing opinions and interpretations
Time - 5 minutes
Preparation - None

1. At the beginning of every class, put one of these quotes up on the board (or find some other quotes you like better):

"It takes courage to be creative. Just as soon as you have a new idea, you are a minority of one." - E. Paul Torrance

"A mind once stretched by a new idea never regains its original dimensions." - Oliver Wendell Holmes

"The unexamined life is not worth living." – Socrates

"There are two ways to slide easily through life; to believe everything or to doubt everything. Both ways save us from thinking." – Alfred Korzybski

"Life consists of what a man is thinking of all day." - Ralph Waldo Emerson

"A problem well-defined is half solved." - John Dewey

"I can't understand why people are frightened of new ideas. I'm frightened of the old ones." - John Cage

"The significant problems we have cannot be solved at the same level of thinking with which we created them." – Albert Einstein

"It is the mark of an educated mind to be able to entertain a thought without accepting it." – Aristotle

"Memory is a complicated thing, a relative to the truth, but not its twin." - Barbara Kingsolver

"An invasion of armies can be resisted, but not an idea whose time has come." - Victor Hugo

"Thinking is the most unhealthy thing in the world, and people die of it just as they die of any other disease." - Oscar Wilde

2. Invite a student to read out the quote. Then ask another student to read it again. Call on someone to explain it.

3. Ask two students for their opinion of the quote. Do they agree with it?

Variations:

- leave a few letters missing from some of the words, and tell students to fill in the blanks.

- leave a few words missing, then call out the words and ask students to write them in the proper places.

- add a couple of errors (grammatical, spelling, semantic, or logical) to the quote and challenge your class to find them and correct them.

- challenge a student to recall a quote from a previous lesson.

1.5 Lateral thinking puzzles

Aims - Listening, guessing, asking questions
Time - 15 minutes
Preparation - None

1. Read one of the following stories to the class without reading the solution:

PUZZLE #1 - Philip's mother requested that he take her to the airport to greet his Aunt Agnes, who was arriving from London, England. Philip's mother and Aunt Agnes had just recently gotten in touch, and they were separated at birth. Philip was concerned that he wouldn't recognize his aunt, as they had never met, and they had never seen each other's pictures. Also, Philip's mother hadn't seen Agnes since they were babies. However, Philip's mother said, "Don't worry, Philip. I'm absolutely sure you will recognize her." Why is she so sure?

Solution: Agnes and Philip's mother are identical twins.

PUZZLE #2 - Three ladies each have two daughters. They have dinner at an elegant restaurant. Even though there are only 7 chairs at their table, everyone is able to sit down in a chair, without adding any extra chairs. How is this so?

Solution: The seven ladies are a grandmother, her two daughters, and their two daughters.

PUZZLE #3 - A boy threw a ball very hard and it came back. However, it didn't hit anything, nobody caught it, and it wasn't tied to anything. How did it happen?

Solution: He threw it straight up over his head.

PUZZLE #4 - A man walks out of his motel room, goes into his car, honks the horn, then goes back to his room. Why?

Solution: It's very late at night. After leaving the motel room, the man forgets which room he is staying in. His wife is deaf, so he honks his horn, thus waking up all the other motel tenants and causing them to turn on their lights. He goes to the room that is still dark.

PUZZLE #5 - A man attended a party and drank several glasses of punch, then left early. Everyone else at the party who drank the punch died. Why did the man survive?

Solution: The ice cubes were poisoned. At the time the man drank the punch, the cubes were still frozen. Later the ice cubes melted, poisoning the punch.

2. After reading, allow students to ask you questions. However, you will only answer yes/no questions. If they have a hard time guessing, you can give them a hint.

Note: If you would like more of these puzzles, do a search on the Internet for lateral thinking puzzles.

1.6 Riddles

Aims - Reading, speaking, guessing
Time - Variable
Preparation - None

1. At the beginning of class, write one of these riddles on the board without the answer:

What is the shortest month?
May. It only has 3 letters.

What gets wet when drying?
A towel.

What belongs to you, but others use it more than you do?
Your name.

What is full of holes, but can hold water?
A sponge.

The more you take, the more you leave behind. What are they?
Footsteps.

The more you take away, the larger it gets. What is it?
A hole.

What can you catch but not throw?
A cold.

What goes around the world but stays in a corner?
A stamp.

2. Announce to the class that the question is a riddle. Tell them you will give them until the end of class to guess the answer.

3. Continue with your lesson. From time to time, invite students to guess the answer.

4. If no one has guessed the answer by the end of class, tell them.

Note: if your class enjoys riddles, you might consider using them on a regular basis.

1.7 Thinking posters

Aims – Writing, reading, individual expression
Time – 30 minutes
Preparation – Bring to class four large sheets of paper, tape and pens

1. Ask students to identify several types of thinking. (Some possibilities are worries, fantasies, dreams, plans, hopes, memories.) Write them on the board.

2. Choose four of them and write each one at the top of a large sheet of paper. Ask students to help you think of a couple of sentence starters to add to the top. (For example, on a page labeled MEMORIES, you might add "I can never forget..." or "My favorite memory of my mother is...")

3. Put the posters up on different walls of the room. Ask students to stand up and write sentences on the posters. Emphasize that each student must write at least a couple of sentences. Also, point out that they should write about the topic at the top of the page, but they don't have to use the word or the sentence starters.

4. Next, get the students to circulate and add a few comments to their classmates' sentences, such as "I feel the same way" or "That's interesting."

5. When students are sitting down again, move around to each poster and read out a few sentences from each one, providing comments both on language and content.

1.8 Thought balloons

Aims – Using pictures to elicit language, writing, speaking, listening
Time - 30 minutes
Preparation – Prepare five or six pictures of people. For best results, use a mix of different ages, races, and facial expressions.

1. At the beginning of class, tape the pictures on the board. Say to the class "I wonder what they're thinking." Point to the first picture and call on a few students to make suggestions.

2. Next call on students to come to the board and draw a balloon above the person's head and write a thought in the balloon. The thought can be funny, unusual or serious.

3. Put students into pairs and ask them to prepare a short skit, where one student silently performs a few actions and the other says aloud what the first student is thinking.

4. Ask several pairs to perform their skit for the whole class.

Variation: To make this a little more complex, you can use pictures of two people and ask students to write both speech balloons and thought balloons for each person, perhaps showing an interesting contrast between the two. This can be developed into a dialogue.

1.9 The language of thinking

Aims – Listening, writing, reading, learning about students' lives, using new vocabulary

Time - 30 minutes

Preparation - Make a list of five or six words and phrases that relate to thinking. For lower level classes, your list might include *guess*, *imagine*, *remember*, and *reflect*. For higher level classes, you could include *ponder*, *weigh the alternatives*, *consider my options*. Prepare to tell the class a story about one time that you did some thinking and made a decision or solved a problem. (Some suggestions: your decision to move to a new city, to get married, or choosing your major in college.) The story should include the words and phrases on your list.

1. In class, write the words and phrases up on the board and tell the class your story.

2. Have students write a few sentences using the new words and phrases. Call on some students to read out their sentences.

3. Ask each student to write a short paragraph (four to five sentences) using the words you taught them, but leaving a blank for each "thinking" word.

4. Put students into pairs and ask them to exchange papers. They must try to fill in the blanks, then return the paragraphs to their partners who will check their work.

1.10 Lost in thought

Aims – Writing, organizing notes, fluency practice, discussion
Time - 20 minutes
Preparation – Make copies of the questions. Draw a large circle or a spiral on the board.

1. Tell students to stare at the shape on the board without talking.

2. Tell them to allow their thoughts to drift. (You might want to play some peaceful music.)

3. After two minutes, get their attention and tell them to write their thoughts down.

4. Repeat steps 1-3 two more times.

5. Now tell students to categorize their thoughts any way they want to (fantasies, memories, worries, plans, etc.)

6. Put students in pairs and ask them to share their thoughts.

7. Now give students copies of the questions below. Organize students into groups of three or four to discuss these questions:

Which categories were the most common? Why?
Do you have a tendency to think a certain way?
Do you have different thoughts at different times of the day?
Tell your classmates about a common thought you have.
Would you describe your thoughts as positive or negative?
Do you use self-talk to change your thoughts? (For example, telling yourself to calm down when you're upset.)
Do you think self-talk is effective? Why or why not?

8. Finally, ask several students to come to the board and write a sentence based on their discussion. (For example, "I'm always thinking about lunch after 11:00." or "I worry too much".)

1.11 It made me think

Aims – Listening, writing, sharing information, guessing
Time - 30 minutes
Preparation – Think of a book, a song or a movie that has somehow influenced your thinking. Prepare to tell the class about it.

1. Ask students to think of a book, a song, or a movie that greatly influenced their thinking. Give them an example from your own life.

2. Pass out index cards and ask them to write down the title of the work in English. Tell them not to write their names. Give them a few minutes to think and write.

3. Tell the class you are going to play a guessing game. You are going to read out the title on the card, and the class must guess who wrote it.

4. Collect the cards and read the first one out. Ask the class to guess who might have written it. Finally ask the writer to identify him or herself, and explain his or her choice.

5. Repeat the activity with the other cards.

1.12 Hindrances to thinking

Aims – Reading, speaking, discussion
Time - 1 hour
Preparations – Make copies of handouts.

1. Ask students to consider their thinking habits. Put them in pairs and ask them to discuss one example of a good thinking habit and one example of a bad thinking habit.

2. Tell the class that Vincent Ryan Ruggiero, an expert on critical thinking, has made a list of some common habits that have a negative effect on the quality of one's thinking. Give them the following handout:

---

6 Habits Which Hinder Thinking

1) mine-is-better – thinking that one's own ideas and values are better than others simply because they are one's own
2) face saving – making excuses or rationalizing after one has made a mistake or done something wrong
3) resistance to change – rejecting new thoughts without making the effort to evaluate them fairly
4) conformity – suspending your own thought processes and agreeing with others
5) overgeneralizing – ascribing to all members of a group characteristics that may apply only to some
6) self-deception – not being honest with yourself

source: *The Art of Thinking* by Vincent Ryan Ruggiero (Longman)

---

3. Give students a few minutes to read.

4. Pass out copies of the discussion questions. Put students into groups of 4 or 5 to discuss.

Discussion Questions

Think of an example of each habit.
Which of these habits is the most harmful?
Which is the most common?
Do you know anyone who has one of these habits? Tell the group about this person.
Do you have any of these habits? Explain.
Can you think of any ways to break these habits?
Can you think of any additional negative thinking habits?
What is an example of a positive thinking habit?

---

5. Now put students into 6 groups. Assign each group a different habit and ask each group to create a role play that demonstrates the habit. Give them at least 15 minutes to prepare.

6. Call on each group to perform their role play for the class.

1.13 Thinking pie chart

Aims - Interviewing, listening, speaking, writing, getting acquainted, guessing
Time - 30 minutes
Preparation – Prepare a pie chart of your everyday thoughts. The categories on your chart might be vague (worrying, spacing out, concentrating, planning) or more specific (thinking about this week's lessons, making plans for the weekend).

1. On the board, draw your pie chart. Explain each section to your students, and encourage them to ask you questions.

2. Put students in pairs. Have each student interview a classmate about his or her thoughts. Then instruct them to make an appropriate pie chart for each other, without writing the student's name.

3. Have students put their pie charts up on the walls.

4. Ask students to wander around and look at the pie charts. Tell them you want them to guess which pie chart belongs to which student.

5. After students are back in their seats, go to a pie chart and read it out, adding your own comments. Call on one or two students to guess whose pie chart it is, before asking the subject of the chart to reveal himself or herself. Repeat with the other pie charts.

Variation: Put students in groups of five or six and have them create a thinking pie chart for a famous person. Ask each group to present their chart to the class. Call on several students to guess who the chart is about.

1.14 When Woody met Wilde

Aims – Reading, matching parts of a sentence, speaking, listening
Time - 2 class periods (1st class period, 20 minutes - 2nd class period, 15 minutes)
Preparation - Bring pictures of Woody Allen and Oscar Wilde to class. Choose 6 of the Allen/Wilde quotes from below (3 from each person), write them on slips of paper, and cut up each quote into 2 parts.

1. As class begins, put the pictures of Oscar Wilde and Woody Allen on the blackboard.

2. Give each student part of a quote. Ask students to mingle in order to find the other half. Next, they need to put the completed quotes up on the board next to the person they think said it.

3. When they are finished, correct any mistakes, and write the names above the pictures. Ask students if they know anything about these two people. (You might want to tell them about both people. Woody Allen is a film director from the United States. He has directed over 30 films, including Manhattan and Annie Hall. Oscar Wilde was an Irish writer who was famous for his plays and novels including The Importance of Being Earnest and The Picture of Dorian Gray.)

4. Call on a few students to read out a quote from the board, and then provide their own interpretation.

5. Ask the entire class to take a vote on the best quote.

6. For homework, ask students to go to one of these websites and find a quote they like:

Cool Quotes - www.coolquotes.com
Quotations at Bartleby.com - www.bartleby.com/quotations
Quotes of the Day - www.qotd.org
Thinkexist.com - www.thinkexist.com
Wikiquote - en.wikiquote.org

Alternatively, students can think of a favorite saying or quote in their own language and translate it into English.

7. In the next class period, ask students to stand up and mingle. They should talk to at least three other people and share their quote.

8. After a few minutes, invite them to return to their seats. Call on a few students to read out a quote someone else told them.

Quotes from Woody Allen:

"My one regret in life is that I am not someone else."

"Man consists of two parts, his mind and his body, only the body has more fun."

"There are worse things in life than death. Have you ever spent an evening with an insurance salesman?"

"Most of the time I don't have much fun. The rest of the time I don't have any fun at all."

"You can live to be a hundred if you give up all the things that make you want to live to be a hundred."

"Life doesn't imitate art, it imitates bad television."

Quotes from Oscar Wilde:

"Always forgive your enemies; nothing annoys them so much."

"I am not young enough to know everything."

"If there was less sympathy in the world, there would be less trouble in the world."

"Education is an admirable thing, but it is well to remember from time to time that nothing that is worth knowing can be taught."

"The only way to get rid of a temptation is to yield to it."

"One can always be kind to people about whom one cares nothing."

1.15 Memory and imagination

Aims - Fluency practice, describing memories, using imagination, speaking, listening
Time - 15 minutes
Preparation – Bring a bell to class.

1. Write the words "memory" and "imagination" up on the board.

2. Tell students to close their eyes and recall something that happened recently.

3. After 2 minutes, ring a bell and then ask them to imagine different parts of the memory changing, such as people, words, images, location, etc.

4. After another 2 minutes, ring the bell again and ask them to change the memory back to what really happened.

5. Repeat steps 3 and 4 a few times, then tell students to open their eyes.

6. Invite students to tell the class about their mental journey.

1.16 Great thinkers

Aims – Writing, asking questions, fluency practice, speaking, listening, note-taking, guessing
Time - 45 minutes
Preparation – Bring a stack of index cards, at least 7 for each student

1. Put a chair at the front of the class. Give each student 7 index cards.

2. Tell the class to imagine there is a great thinker, a very wise person in the chair. They need to write down several questions, one on each card, to ask the great thinker.

3. After 10 minutes, collect the cards and shuffle them. Call on a student to sit in the chair. This student will act as the great thinker. Suggest that the student invent a new name, and list a few of his or her achievements for the class.

4. Call on another student to come up to the front, choose a card, and read it to the student in the chair. The student in the chair will answer in the role of the great thinker. Tell the rest of the class to take notes. They should write down the two most important statements of the great thinker. Call on two other students to draw cards and ask the great thinker some questions. Next, replace the great thinker with another student.

5. Repeat steps 3 and 4 several times until most of the students have participated.

6. Now have all the students return to their seats. Read out a few more questions, and ask students to write down what they think the great thinker would respond with.

7. When they are finished writing, call on a few students to read their answers to the questions.

8. Next, call on a student to come to the board and draw a frame. Ask the student to draw a picture of one of the great thinkers in your class, and write a quote from the thinker below it, without identifying the student. Ask the class to guess who it is. Repeat twice.

1.17 Creative and critical thinking

Aims – Listening, writing, discussion, speaking, expressing opinions, summarizing
Time - 30 minutes
Preparation – Prepare copies of the discussion questions

1. At the start of class, write a big heading on the board with CREATIVE THINKING on the left and CRITICAL THINKING on the right.

2. Ask students copy the heading from the board onto their paper.

3. Dictate the following words and phrases, and instruct students to put them in the column they think is most appropriate:

Brainstorming
Being practical
Choosing a plan
Coming up with ideas
Fantasizing
Generating a wide range of solutions
Narrowing down options
Deciding
Selecting the best idea
Judging
Thinking of several options
Using your imagination

4. Next, invite one student to come to the board, and take over your role. This student's task is to call on students to read out their answers as he or she writes them in the proper column.

5. Point out any errors in spelling or grammar. Ask students if they think any of the words or phrases should be moved to the other column.

6. Call on a few students to tell you what they think is the major difference between creative thinking and critical thinking.

7. Hand out copies of these discussion questions. Assign students to discuss the questions in groups of four or five:

> Do you think you are better at creative thinking or critical thinking? Why?
> Which of the two skills would you like to improve? Think of at least 2 ways to do this.
> Are these two types of thinking supportive friends or hostile enemies? Explain your answer.
> Is creativity valued in your country? What about critical thinking?
> Recall the last time you did something creative. Describe it to your group.
> Can you think of a situation where your critical thinking skills came into play? Tell the group about it.
> What famous person would you describe as creative? Who would you say is a good critical thinker?

8. Ask each group to relay the highlights of their discussion to the class.

Possible answers:

Creative thinking – brainstorming, coming up with ideas, generating a wide range of solutions, fantasizing, thinking of several options, using your imagination

Critical thinking – being practical, choosing a plan, narrowing down options, deciding, selecting the best idea, judging

1.18 Thinking styles

Aims - Speaking, listening, discussing
Time - 1.5 hours
Preparation – None

1. Call on students to list several types of thinking. Write these on different parts of the board. They might include creative thinking, logical thinking, rational thinking, as well as others.

2. Tell students that you want them to imagine that they are psychologists. You will put them into groups of 4 or 5, and each group must come up with a list of 4 thinking styles based on categories you give them. Each group will have a different category. For example, if you give a group the category "shapes", they might come up with oval thinking, triangle thinking, square thinking, and circle thinking. If you give another group the category "animals", they might come up with pig thinking, dog thinking, cat thinking, and monkey thinking. The group needs to write down a list of the 4 thinking styles, along with an explanation of each.

3. When all groups are finished, they must put together an 8 item psychological test that will test people for their most dominant thinking skill. Each item should be a multiple choice question, and the test must include a scoring system which tells the user his or her dominant thinking style.

4. Assign each group to put their test on a large sheet of paper and put it up on the wall when they're finished.

5. Invite all students to circulate and take one or two of the tests.

6. Get a few students to share with the class their thinking style according to one of the tests. Do the other students agree?

Variation: Ask groups to exchange lists after step 2.

1.19 Reading - "Master the Art of Making Meaning"

Aims – Reading, writing, discussion, speaking, listening, using imperatives, using the structure "You wouldn't ...would you?"
Time – 1.5 hours
Preparation – Make copies of the article and discussion questions

1. Preteach the following vocabulary: interpretation, circumstances, jerk, postulate, puberty

2. Ask students what they would do if they were parking a car, and someone took the parking space they were about to use. Put students in pairs and ask them to describe what they would think and say. Call on a few students to share their responses.

3. Tell the class they are about to read an article which suggests one course of action in this type of situation.

4. Give students copies of the article, and allow time for them to read.

5. Hand out copies of the following questions. Put students in groups of three or four to discuss:

> Do you agree with the author that the mind is a "meaning-making machine"? Why or why not?
> What automatic interpretations have you made since you started taking this class?
> Have you ever made an interpretation that turned out to be completely wrong? Give an example.
> Look at the situations below and see if your group can come up with 3 different interpretations for each:
>
> Your sister doesn't wear the bracelet you bought her for her birthday.

> A stranger on the bus gives you an unfriendly look.
> Someone bumps into you on the sidewalk and walks away without saying anything.
> A classmate stops saying "good morning" to you.

6. Read out the situations from the handout, and call on students to give you some of their interpretations. Write their interpretations on the board, pointing out any grammatical errors.

7. Ask students to underline these parts of the article:

Challenge yourself.
Don't settle for the first interpretation that comes to mind.
Say to yourself...

Call on a student to tell you the subject of these sentences. (Answer: you – the reader). Tell the class that this is the imperative form. It is more direct and has more impact than saying "I think you should challenge yourself." or "In my opinion, I feel you should say to yourself..."

8. Now tell the class to imagine there is a student who is very worried about an exam. Ask students to write down three things they could say to get him to calm down, using the imperative. Have students work in pairs to compare their sentences.

9. Ask one student to read out a sentence, and choose another student to come up with a more indirect version.

10. Ask students to circle the following questions from the article:

You wouldn't marry the first person you met after puberty, would you?
You wouldn't take a job at the first place you saw a "Help Wanted" sign, would you?

Explain that the author is using this type of question to persuade the reader to agree with him. Give students this example: your best friend has started smoking, so you say to him: "You wouldn't want to get lung cancer, would you?" or "You wouldn't want to stink of cigarettes all day, would you?"

11. Tell students you would like to them to think of another situation where someone might want to persuade another person to do or not to do something. Give them a few minutes to think of a situation and write it down.

12. Call on a student to come to the front of the class and read out the situation, then choose a student to come up with an appropriate response, using the "You wouldn't......would you?" structure. Repeat two or three times.

———

Master the Art of Making Meaning
by Adam Khan

Your mind is a meaning-making machine. Without even trying, you "know" what things mean, at least most of the time. When someone treats you rudely, your mind interprets that. It makes some meaning out of it. And it's completely automatic. That is, you don't stop and think about it. You don't *try* to make an interpretation. It happens without any effort on your part.

The meanings you make affect the way you feel and determine how you interact with people and circumstances. The interpretations you make about the events in your life have a significant influence on the amount of stress you experience in your day.

For example, let's say someone cuts you off on the freeway. And let's further postulate, just for fun, that your automatic interpretation is "What a jerk." The interpretation would probably make you upset, at least a little bit. But realize that it doesn't feel like you're making the *interpretation* "What a jerk." The way it feels to you is that your assessment of the person is obvious, and anyone in their right mind would make the same assessment in the same circumstances. But believe it or not, your interpretation was your own doing, and it wasn't the only possible interpretation you could have made.

The important thing about this is that your interpretations change the way you feel, *and those feelings change the way you interact with the world.*

The good news is: You're not stuck with the interpretations your mind makes automatically. You can come up with new ones. You wouldn't marry the first person you met after puberty, would you? You wouldn't take a job at the first place you saw a "Help Wanted" sign, would you? Well, you don't have to use the first interpretation that pops into your head, either.

In the example above, the possible ways to interpret someone cutting you off are virtually unlimited. How about this one: The person had unexpected car trouble and now is running terribly late to an important appointment. If the driver is a woman, maybe she's in labor and needs to get to a hospital *now*. If it's a man, maybe he was called at work and told his wife is in labor. Maybe his brakes went out. Maybe he's having heart trouble.

None of those interpretations are better than any others in an absolute way. But which one leaves you able to go on about your day feeling fine? Or, if it's a situation that keeps repeating itself and requires action, which interpretation will make you most effective at dealing with that situation?

Challenge yourself. Don't settle for the first interpretation that comes to mind. Say to yourself, "Okay, it might mean that...what else could it mean? What's another way to interpret this?" You will feel better, treat people better, and handle situations better. Do you know what this could mean to you? You tell me.

Come up with alternative ways of interpreting an event.

http://www.youmeworks.com/mastertheartofmakingmeaning.html

———

Further Reading

Books

Crawford, A., Saul, E. W., Mathews, S. R., and Makinster, J. 2005. *Teaching and learning strategies for the thinking classroom*. New York: The International Debate Education Association.

Cowley, S. 2004. *Getting the buggers to think*. London: Continuum.

Websites

The Thinking Approach Project
http://www.thinking-approach.org/

The Standards Site: Thinking Skills in Primary Classrooms
http://www.standards.dfes.gov.uk/thinkingskills/

2
Memory

This chapter contains a variety of activities all related to the theme of memory. Many activities here directly address language learning and how to learn new vocabulary. In addition this chapter also includes memory games and activities for sharing positive memories.

STAGES OF THE MEMORY PROCESS

There are three stages of the memory process: learning, storing, and retrieving. In the first stage, you focus on a piece of information you want to remember. In the second stage, you keep the information in your head until it is later needed. In the third stage, you recall the information again at a later date. All three stages are important for learning.

TWO TYPES OF MEMORY

There are two main types of memory: short-term memory and long-term memory. You use short-term memory to store pieces of information you only need for a few seconds, such as a phone number you just looked up. Storage is limited for short-term memory. Long-term memory has almost unlimited storage and handles things that you remember for longer periods of time including skills (procedural memory), facts (semantic memory), and personal experiences (episodic memory).

In order to transfer information from short-term memory to long-term memory, you must manipulate the information and play around with it. This takes place in working memory, also known as the mental workbench. In reference to language teaching, Stevick (1998) states "we need to find out how to select the short-term memory items we're interested in...and then devise effective techniques for converting those items into long-term memories." The activities in this chapter suggest a number of ways of doing this. (See Stevick's *Memory Meaning and Method* for an extended discussion of memory and language learning.)

COGNITIVE RESEARCH ON MEMORY

Sharifian (2002) summarizes cognitive research on memory enhancement that have direct relevance to language learning. He points out 10 effects that could improve retention of language.

1. The generation effect – students are more likely to recall vocabulary that they partially or completely generate on their own. One example would be asking students to fill in the missing letters of words in a story, rather than simply reading the complete text.

2. The isolation effect – students can remember vocabulary better if they have been presented a word in combination with other words that are similar to each other, but different from the chosen word. For example, in the list DOG CAT PIG BOOK MONKEY, the word book would be remembered more easily.

3. The time-of-day effect – students are likely to remember different types of vocabulary better at different times of day. Surface linguistic forms are better remembered if learned in the morning, and semantic features are better for the afternoon.

4. The serial-position effect – students will usually remember the first items on a list the best and the last items second best. These are called, respectively, the primacy effect and the recency effect. The items in the middle are the hardest to recall.

5. The spacing effect – students tend to learn better when repetitions of material are spaced out.

6. The modality effect – auditory presentation has been shown to have a better effect on recall than visual presentation. However, a combination of two modes (visual and auditory) has also been shown to work better than using only one mode.

7. The self-reference effect – students usually pick up vocabulary better if they use it in reference to themselves, rather than other people or objects.

8. The bizarreness effect – students are likely to have better recall of sentences that are bizarre or unusual.

9. The encoding-context effect – students remember material better if they are taught and tested in the same environment.

10. The processing-difficulty effect – students are more likely to remember vocabulary that takes more time to process. For example, if students encounter a sentence containing an unexpected word that makes them slow down, they will be more likely to remember that word.

Some of these effects are easier to apply to a language teaching context than others. For example, most teachers don't have a great deal of control over what time of day they teach or what room they teach in, but they can incorporate spaced repetition into their lessons or provide opportunities to personalize new vocabulary.

TIPS FOR HELPING STUDENTS REMEMBER

Here are some suggestions that you can use everyday in class to help your students move more words and phrases into long-term memory:

Meaning - Make sure that students are aware of the meaning of new vocabulary, even if you need to use their mother tongue.

Association - Give students opportunities to relate something new they are learning to what they already know.

Visualization - Students will learn vocabulary better if they can associate words with images, especially if the images are vivid and involve some degree of movement. Humorous, absurd, exaggerated images are recommended. Oxford (1990) points out several good reasons for making connections between words and images: "First, the mind's storage capacity for visual information exceeds its capacity for verbal material. Second, the most efficiently packaged chunks of information are transferred to long-term memory through visual images. Third, visual images may be the most potent device to aid recall of verbal material. Fourth, a large proportion of learners have a preference for visual learning." (p. 40).

Collocations and chunks - Provide collocations and chunks containing words they are learning, or assign students to find them for homework.

Keyword technique – One well-known technique for learning vocabulary is the keyword technique. Students focus on an English word, think of a similar sounding word in their first language, and develop a mental image that incorporates both words. However, as Hulstijn (1997) points out, "it can be successfully applied with only a minority of language items...words referring to objects that can be perceived visually" (p. 220).

Organization - Tell students to organize new words and phrases on paper. They can organize words into categories, or make a chart of the ideas they read about in a text. Mind-mapping is another option. There are now several websites which allow users to create mind-maps online, such as Text2Mindmap (www.text2mindmap.com), which turns a list of words into a mind-map.

Rhyme - Have students create rhymes using new words and familiar words. Assign them to write a song, a rhyme, a rap, or a grammar chant.

Testing - Provide time for students to test themselves and each other on how much they have learned so far. Some classes take great pleasure in coming up with challenging questions. Make sure they use a mix of different question types, including true or false, multiple choice, fill-in-the-blank, short answer and open answer.

Review - At given intervals, review some of the language you want students to retain. They should review language in new contexts (use language from a news article in a role play or write a poem using words from a film clip they watched).

———

2.1 The name game

Aims – Learning names, getting acquainted, speaking, listening, fluency practice
Time - 1 class period
Preparation – Purchase a small prize. Prepare handouts with a layout of your classroom, with a box for each seat.

Note: This activity is intended for the first class period, when students are still learning each other's names.

1. At the beginning of class, challenge students to learn each other's names. Tell them you will give a prize to the student who learns the most names. Give them these suggestions for learning names:

- ask the person to say his or her name again slowly
- repeat the name several times in your mind
- use the name a few times (Nice to meet you, Bill...Are you new here, Bill?)
- ask the person some questions about the name (How do you spell your name? What does it mean? Is that a common name in your country?)
- if possible, think of an image suggested by the name
- visualize the person's name in bright letters in front of his or her face
- think of a word that rhymes with the name
- think of a word in your language that sounds similar to the name
- find a distinguishing feature of the person's appearance (tall, big ears, etc.) and associate it with the name

2. Ask them to walk around and mingle. They should talk briefly to each classmate, then sit down when they have met everyone.

3. Continue the lesson and at the end of class, ask "How many names do you remember?" Pass out the handouts and ask students to write the names of their classmates in the boxes. The first person to fill in all the names correctly wins the prize.

Follow-up: You can get students to use these techniques to learn the names of the teachers and office staff at your school.

2.2 Classic memory techniques

Aims – Listening, reviewing, learning vocabulary, speaking
Time - 30 minutes
Preparation - Prepare a list of words and examples for the methods in step 2.

1. Give students a few minutes to look through their coursebooks and find 8 names of objects, preferably ones they haven't mastered yet. Have them write the words down.

2. Introduce students to these three methods of learning words:

Roman room method – Imagine the different parts of your room. Associate each word with a different place in the room (the bed, the door, the window).

Story method – Visualize a story which involves each of the items on your list. Begin the story with the first item, and have it interact with the second item. Continue until you reach the end of your list.

Journey method – Picture a familiar route, such as the trip you take to school. Associate each item on your list with a particular place on the journey.

3. Give students an example of how you might use each method to remember a few words.

4. Give students about 10 minutes to choose a method and then close their eyes and use their preferred method to remember the objects on their list.

5. Next, have students choose a partner, and exchange lists. Each student should try to recall their words, without looking at the list. Then they should describe the technique they used, and how they learned each item.

Variations:

- Use items from a picture dictionary instead of the coursebook.
- Get students to make shopping lists, and use one of the methods to memorize the items on their lists.

2.3 Sense-memory-fantasy technique

Aims – Speaking, describing
Time – 20 minutes
Preparation – None

1. Ask students to tell you some vocabulary they have learned recently that they want to remember. Write the words on the board as students call them out. Stop when you have about 12 words.

2. Now tell students you want to introduce them to a memory technique that will help them remember the words. Tell them to choose 5 and associate each one with a sense, a memory, and a fantasy. They should make these associations vivid and detailed. For example, the word cinnamon could be associated with the smell of a cinnamon roll (sense), a memory of cooking with cinnamon, and a fantasy of the teacher's desk being covered with a huge pile of cinnamon. Give students time to use the technique.

3. Invite a student to read out a word from the list and share his or her associations with the class. Repeat this step with 4 more students.

2.4 How we learn new words

Aims – Speaking, listening, fluency practice, sharing of learning strategies
Time - 20 minutes
Preparation – None

1. Ask students to think of how they learn new words and phrases. For example, they might think of writing words down on index cards, using the words in a conversation, or looking up words in a dictionary.

2. Put students into pairs and ask them to brainstorm at least 5 ways to learn new words.

3. After 5 minutes, put students into different pairs and get them to think of 2 more ways.

4. Now ask students to come up to the board and write down one way to memorize new words that came up in their discussion.

5. End the activity by sharing some of the tips from the beginning of this chapter.

Follow-up: For homework, you can assign students to find additional ways from sources outside the classroom.

2.5 Learning phrases

Aims – Review, listening, speaking
Time - 20 minutes
Preparation – None

1. At the beginning of class, write on the blackboard 5 or 6 phrases that you want students to review.

2. In class, point to the first phrase. Read it out and ask students to say it.

3. Now tell your students to close their eyes and imagine one of their previous teachers standing in front of them saying the phrase three times.

4. Next tell them to close their eyes again and imagine a tourist from their own country in a country where the target language is spoken, saying the phrase in an appropriate situation.

5. Finally, have them close their eyes one more time and imagine themselves saying the phrase in some situation where they would need to use it.

6. Ask students to repeat steps 3-5 with all the phrases on the board until they have finished all of them.

7. Erase all the phrases on the board. Say one or two keywords from the first phrase, and challenge a student to recall the entire phrase. Continue with the other phrases.

2.6 Memory lapses

Aims – Fluency practice, speaking, listening, summarizing, reading
Time - 30 minutes
Preparation – Make copies of the handout.

1. Put students in pairs and ask them to think of 3 things people usually forget. After a few minutes, call on several students to tell you their answers.

2. Now write the following sentences in different places on the board:

"I can't remember where I left my keys!"
"It's so hard to remember people's names!"
"I forgot my password again."
"I never can remember my mother's birthday."
"Sometimes I walk into a room, and then can't remember why I went there."
"When I park my car in a large parking lot, I can't find it later."

3. Put students in groups of four or five. Tell them to think of at least 2 solutions for each of the memory problems.

4. When they're finished, read out each statement and call on several students to tell the class some of their solutions.

5. Then give students this handout of solutions for the problems:

Solutions to Common Memory Problems

If you often forget where you put your keys, describe your actions out loud. Say "I'm putting my keys in the purple ashtray." Another idea is to always put your keys in the same place.

Here's some advice for remembering names. When you meet someone new, think of the name and create a clever pun or mnemonic to help you remember it. For example, if you meet a tall man named Jim, you might think of a very tall "gym". Also, repeat the name several times in your head, and use it in conversation, as in "Very nice to meet you, Jim."

You can remember your passwords better if you give the numbers a meaning. Look at the digits and associate them with important numbers you already know, such as your birthday, your address or your phone number.

The best solution for remembering important birthdays and anniversaries is to get an organizer or a PDA to record important dates. You can also use the calendar or organizer function on your cell phone.

Another common memory problem is forgetting why you went into a room. Before you go to another room, picture what you want to get or do. Make a strong, vivid image. If you enter a room and can't remember what you were planning to do there, you can try to remember what you were thinking and feeling before you arrived and that can help you recall your motive.

If you have trouble remembering where you parked your car in a large parking lot, just tie a brightly colored ribbon to the antenna of your car. Alternatively, you can adopt the habit of parking in the same general area of the parking lot wherever you go.

2.7 Remembering a paragraph

Aims – Review, reading, speaking
Time – 15 minutes
Preparation - None

1. On the board, write a short paragraph from a text you covered recently in class. It should be about 3 to 5 sentences long.

2. Ask one student to read out the paragraph.

3. Next erase 3 or 4 words and ask another student to read out the paragraph, including the missing words.

4. Repeat the previous step until most of the paragraph has been erased.

Variations:

- A more challenging version of this activity is to ask students to work together in groups of four or five to reproduce the paragraph from memory without seeing it on the board. Allow them to look at the paragraph for a minute, and then put their books away. Give them a few minutes to write it out, then ask three groups to write their paragraphs on the board. Finally, ask them to compare their paragraphs with the paragraph in the coursebook.

- Teach students to make a simple paper airplane. The website Alex's Paper Airplanes (www.paperairplanes.co.uk) has some easy-to-follow tutorials. Ask them to choose five keywords from a paragraph, and write them on different parts of the plane. Then ask them to "fly" the airplane to a classmate. The classmate opens the airplane and reconstructs the paragraph based on the keywords, writing the paragraph on the unfolded paper. Then the student folds the paper back into an airplane, and returns it to the first student, who checks the paragraph with the original and gives the second student a grade.

Acknowledgement: I learned about this type of activity from Dave Willis' article, "Techniques for priming and recycling", which can be found on the Teaching English website (www.teachingenglish.org.uk).

2.8 Review posters

Aims – Review, writing, categorizing language
Time - 30 minutes
Preparation – Bring in several large sheets of paper and colored markers.

1. Put students in groups of five. Ask each group to think of 20 to 25 new words and phrases they've picked up recently.

2. Now ask each group to put some of the words and phrases into 4 categories (for example, 3 phrases we'd like to use more often, 3 words that sound good, 3 words that are hard to pronounce.)

3. Give each group some paper and ask them to put their categories and the accompanying lists of words and phrases on a poster. Encourage them to make the poster colorful and visually appealing.

4. When they're finished, ask them to put the posters up on the walls. Go around to each poster and call on students to make sentences with some of the words and phrases.

2.9 PowerPoint review

Aims – Review, listening, answering questions
Time -10 minutes
Preparation - Prepare a PowerPoint presentation that contains 10 to 20 slides. Each slide should feature a word or phrase you want to review with the class, along with a memorable image that relates to the word. You should prepare a brief definition of the word, along with a translation, a sentence and a question to ask your students that uses the word.

1. At the beginning of class, tell students that you are going to give a vocabulary review in the form of a brief PowerPoint presentation. Tell them to write down five words they would like to remember from the presentation.

2. Give your presentation. Ask students your questions as the presentation progresses, and add some follow-up questions.

Variations:

- Assign students to prepare their own PowerPoint reviews to share with the class.

- Try using a Pecha Kucha approach. Pecha Kucha is the name of a type of PowerPoint presentation created by Astrid Klein and Mark Dytham to keep presentations more brief and to the point. The rules are simple: each presenter can use 20 slides, and each slide is shown for 20 seconds. This comes to a total of 6 minutes and 40 seconds. This type of presentation takes slightly more preparation, since the presenter has only 20 seconds to comment on each slide.

2.10 The best sentence competition

Aims – Review, writing sentences, judging sentences
Time - 1 hour
Preparation – None

1. Ask students to rank these three sentences:

Halibut is good.
Halibut is delicious.
I caught a halibut when I went fishing last Saturday.

Which sentence best explains the meaning of the word?

2. Tell students to write down the ideal qualities of a good example sentence.

3. Put them in pairs to compare their lists.

4. Call on several students to tell you their ideas. They might include some of the following:

An example sentence should make the meaning of the word clear without being too long. It helps if the sentence paints a picture or appeals to the senses. In addition, it doesn't hurt if the sentence is clever or funny.

5. Put students in groups of three or four. Ask each group to produce a list of 7 useful words for review.

6. Call on several groups to read out 4 or 5 words from their lists. Write them up on the board, and stop when you have 20.

7. Next tell the class you are going to play a game where they will work in teams to think of a good sentence for some of the words on the board.

8. Choose three students to come to the front of the class. Arrange for them to sit on the side. They will be the judges who will choose the best sentence. Now put the rest of the students into two teams.

9. Circle a word on the board, then give 2 minutes for each group to think up a good sentence. Next, each group sends a student to the front to read out their sentence. Give the judges a couple of minutes to choose the superior sentence. They announce the winning team and explain why they chose their sentence. The winning team gets one point.

10. Continue the game until one team has 10 points, or when there are no more words on the board.

2.11 Dyadic circles review

Aims – Review, writing questions, speaking, listening, asking questions, answering questions
Time - 30 minutes
Preparation – Bring index cards to class.

1. Tell students to review their notes and coursebooks. Ask them to write 6 questions about the previous week's material, using some new vocabulary. The first three questions should be straightforward, and the other three should be more creative. For example, after a unit on shopping, a straightforward question would be "What is your favorite local shop?" or "Do you like shopping on the weekend?" while a more creative question would be "If you owned a shop, what color would you paint the walls?" or "How many people do you think would fit in the shop across the street?"

2. Give each student an index card. Ask each student to pick his or her two best questions, and write them on the card, one on each side.

3. Next, instruct students to take their cards and stand in two circles, one inside the other. The two circles should face each other, so that everyone is standing in front of a partner. (Note: if you have one extra student, you can either join the activity yourself, or assign the extra student to help you make sure the activity is going smoothly.)

4. Students will take turns reading one question from their card, asking their partner, and listening to the response. When a pair is finished, they should raise their hands. When all students have their hands raised, tell the students in the outer circle to move down one. Now everyone has a new partner.

5. Repeat the previous step four or five times.

Variations:

- you can ask students to exchange their cards after a couple of turns, so they get to ask a greater variety of questions

- in step 2, you can give students 3 cards to write questions on, and turn them into you. You give each student a card written by another student. After a couple of turns, give them the option of getting a new card from you, or continuing with the same card.

2.12 Recycling a song

Aims – Review, writing, reading, singing
Time - 30 minutes
Preparation – None

1. Ask one student to come to the board. The student should call on classmates to read out some new words and phrases they have learned during the last few lessons, and write them on the board.

2. Put them in groups of three, and ask them to think of a song they know well, and they think most of the class will be familiar with. (It doesn't have to be an English song.) Then ask the groups to write new lyrics for the song, including a few words and phrases from the blackboard.

3. Give them 10-15 minutes to write and practice.

4. Call on a few groups to sing to the class.

5. For homework, students can bring copies of their lyrics to the next class to give to their classmates.

2.13 Challenging sentences

Aims – Review, sentence formation
Time – 20 minutes
Preparation – None

1. Ask students to review their notes and coursebook from the past 3 lessons, and find vocabulary they want to remember. Tell students to call out some of their words as you write them on the board. Add additional vocabulary you think they should focus on. Stop when you have about 25-30 words.

2. Explain that you want a student to come to the board, circle two words, then challenge another student to make a sentence using the words. For example, Kenji might circle a couple of words then say "Maria, I challenge you to make a sentence using _____ and _____." When the second student has finished reading out his or her sentence, ask the first student to make some comments. Repeat until most of the vocabulary has been used.

Variation: Students create sentences using two words from the board. A student comes to the front of the class, and reads out his or her sentence, saying "BEEP" instead of the two words from the board. The student then challenges another student to repeat the sentence, guessing which two words from the board go into the blanks. The first student confirms if the second student has guessed correctly or not. Repeat several times.

2.14 Guessing words

Aims – Vocabulary review, guessing
Time – 30 minutes
Preparation – Bring a die and a lot of index cards to class.

1. Give each student four index cards. Ask students to write a new word they've encountered recently on each card.

2. Collect the cards. Divide the class into two teams.

3. Tell students that you are going to play a game. Write the following on the board:

1 - mime the word
2 - translate the word
3 - make a sentence
4 - draw a picture
5 - make a collocation
6 - give a definition

Teams will take turns. A student from each team will come to the front of the classroom, roll the die, take a card, and use the corresponding way of explaining the word on the card. The student cannot use more than one example or one way of explaining the word. Also, the student must NOT use the word or phrase, so if the student rolls a 3 or a 5, he or she must say "blank" where the word should go. If a team cannot guess the word, then the card goes back into the deck. Each time a team gets a word correctly, they get one point.

4. Play until one team gets 10 points.

2.15 Sharing vocabulary

Aims – Review, making sentences, sharing
Time – 45 minutes
Preparation – None

This activity works best with a text or coursebook unit that contains a large number of concrete nouns.

1. Ask students to make a list of concrete nouns covered in the coursebook unit or text. Also, tell students to add articles to nouns that need them (an apple, a TV...)

2. Invite students to come to the board and put a check mark next to any of the nouns that would make a good gift, and put an x next to any nouns that would not.

3. Next, write these sentence patterns on the board:

I would like to give _____ _____ because...
I would like to share _____ with _____ because...
I would like to make _____ insanely happy with _____ because...
I would like to surprise _____ with _____ because...
I would like to ruin _____'s day with _____ because...
I would like to put _____ in a bad mood with _____ because...
I would like to confuse _____ with _____ because...
I would like to hide _____ in _____'s bag because...

Tell students to write 3 sentences, using names of people in the classroom and concrete nouns they wrote earlier. For example, I would like to share a novel with Luigi, because I know he likes to read. Students can follow the sentence patterns on the board or create their own.

4. Give students a few minutes to write. Then call on each student to read out a sentence, encouraging the student whose name is mentioned to respond. Correct any errors.

5. Finally put students in groups of 3 to make a sentence for you. Call on each group to read their sentence.

2.16 Movie trailer quiz

Aims – Describing a film clip, noticing differences, asking questions, answering questions
Time - 45 minutes
Preparation – Go to the Youtube website and find two slightly different movie trailers for a movie that is currently playing in your area, or a movie you think would appeal to your class.

1. Briefly introduce the film that is featured in the movie trailer. Ask the students: Has anyone heard of this film before? Who are the main actors and actresses? Who is the director?

2. Play both trailers for the class. Tell students that you want to play the trailers again, and you want them to prepare five questions about the two trailers for a classmate. (Some examples: Which trailer was shorter? What were the first words you heard in the second trailer? Which trailer featured more narration?)

3. Play both trailers 3 times, and allow time for students to write questions.

4. Put students into pairs and ask them to exchange quizzes. After taking a quiz, the student returns it to the quiz's author who will check the answers.

5. Finally, put students into groups of five. Each group should choose their best question to ask the teacher.

2.17 Do you remember?

Aims – Writing, remembering, discussion
Time - 15 minutes
Preparation – None

1. Before class, write these categories up on the board in capital letters:

THINGS THE TEACHER SAID
THINGS THE STUDENTS SAID
THINGS THE TEACHER DID
THINGS THE STUDENTS DID

2. Put students in groups of three. Ask them to discuss your last class period together, and list a few items for each category on the board.

3. Invite a representative from each group to write one or two items under each category.

4. Once they are finished writing, tell them to add questions they have about other students' comments.

5. Ask several students why they remembered what they did. Then ask others what they will probably remember the most about today's lesson.

2.18 Memory overload

Aims – Skimming, fluency practice, speaking, listening
Time - 30 minutes
Preparation – Bring in copies of brief news articles. You should have a different news item for each student.

1. At the beginning of class, give each student a different news article. Assign each of them to read the article and summarize it in 2 or 3 sentences.

2. Next, collect the articles. Clear out a big space in the center of the room, or take them outside the classroom to an empty area.

3. Ask students to mingle in pairs. They must exchange their summaries verbally, then form a new pair with another student. They will do this several times. However, each time they meet with a different student, they must remember all the previous summaries and exchange them as well. Tell them to sit down when they can no longer remember all the previous summaries, or when they have already interacted with all of their classmates.

4. Ask a few students how many article summaries they remember. Find out who can remember the most, and ask that student to relay them to the class.

2.19 Role plays about memory

Aims – Fluency practice, speaking, listening
Time - 30 minutes
Preparation – None

1. Put students in pairs. Give them one of the following situations for a role play. Suggest that they add a conflict or a surprise to the role play:

A is an amnesiac. B is A's friend. B tries to help A remember who he or she is.

A and B are old friends. They recall events from many years ago, but they always remember the details a little differently.

A is a doctor who can remove some unpleasant memories and enhance more positive memories. B is a patient who has come to receive B's services.

2. After they have practiced the role play for a few minutes, combine pairs into groups of four. Have the pairs perform their role plays for each other, and decide who gave the best performance. The group sends the pair with the best role play to the front of the classroom to perform for the whole class.

2.20 Dictation about memory

Aims – Listening, writing, discussion, speaking
Time - 30 minutes
Preparation – None

1. Tell the class you are going to do a dictation. Instruct students to write the questions (but not the answers) and draw a blank line after the fourth and the eighth questions.

Read out these questions:

What is your favorite childhood memory?
How do you remember things you need to do?
In what situation are you likely to forget something?
What is the earliest memory you can recall?
_____

What is the best way to memorize material for a test?
Can you recall an embarrassing situation where you forgot to do something?
Why are some things easier to remember than others?
Have you ever seen a memory expert on TV?
_____

2. After the dictation, call on students to write the 8 questions on the board. Ask students to point out any errors in spelling, grammar or punctuation.

3. Now give students a few minutes to write two more questions about memory in the blanks on their paper. Circulate and look over the students' questions. Ask a few of them to write their own questions on the board.

4. Put students in groups of four to discuss the questions, including their own questions.

5. At the end of the discussion, call on a few students to tell you some of the answers they heard in their group.

6. Finally, call on a student to read out one of the student-generated questions on the board, and call on another student to answer it. Repeat several times.

2.21 Remembering the past

Aims – Fluency practice, speaking, listening
Time - 15 minutes
Preparation – None

1. Tell students to sit quietly and close their eyes. Ask them to think of a happy memory from the past, such as a time they spent with a close friend, or something that made them laugh a lot. They need to recall as much detail as possible.

2. Put students into pairs and ask them to tell their classmates about the memory. Encourage students who are doing the listening to ask questions to get more information.

3. Ask a few students to tell the class about their memories.

4. Finally, toss out a few yes/no questions to see what their memories had in common. For example, you might ask "Did your memory involve your family?" or "Did it happen on a trip?"

2.22 Vivid memories

Aims – Noticing, speaking. listening, getting acquainted
Time - 15 minutes
Preparation – None

1. Ask the class, "What were you doing when you first heard about the 911 terrorist attack?" or "Where were you when you learned about the death of Princess Diana?" (You can substitute another major event, if there is one you think the students might be more familiar with.) Call on two or three students to tell you what they remember.

2. Tell students that when a major event happens that is rather shocking, we often remember in great detail the moment we heard the news, even many years after the event. This phenomenon is called a flashbulb memory.

3. Tell students you now want them to create a highly detailed memory similar to a flashbulb memory. Put students in pairs, preferably with someone they don't know so well. For two minutes, they should pay attention to each other in great detail and take turns describing what they notice. For example, "I notice that you have a scar on your left hand. I notice that you are wearing a bright blue shirt. I notice that you are sitting up very straight. I notice you keep scratching your nose."

4. Now have them turn around in their chairs and close their eyes. Tell them to imagine their classmate and imagine all the detail they just noticed.

5. Tell students to open their eyes and turn around. Did they miss anything?

6. Ask for a few students to describe their reactions to this activity.

———

For the Teacher

In the following interview, Marilee Sprenger, who has written several books on memory and learning, explains the basics of memory for teachers.

An Interview with Marilee Sprenger

Marilee Sprenger is considered an expert in education on the brain, learning and memory, and differentiation. She is one of the most entertaining and informative authors and speakers in the field of education. She leaves her audiences with practical techniques to implement in their classrooms immediately. Marilee is a member of the American Academy of Neurology, the Learning and the Brain Society, and the Cognitive Neuroscience Society as well as many education organizations such as ASCD and Phi Delta Kappa. She is the author of *Learning and Memory: The Brain in Action, Becoming a Wiz at Brain-based Teaching, Differentiation through Learning Styles and Memory, How to Teach So Students Remember, Memory 101 for Educators*, and *The Developing Brain: Birth through Age Eight*. She has written numerous articles, contributed to textbooks, and provides staff development internationally.

A former classroom teacher, she is an adjunct professor at Aurora University, teaching graduate courses on brain based teaching, learning and memory, differentiation, reading and the brain, and early childhood development. Teachers who have read Marilee's work or heard her speak agree that they walk away with user-friendly information that can be applied at all levels.

How did you first get interested in the subject of memory?

Two situations prompted my interest in memory. First, as I age I find myself forgetting little things. I was concerned about how and why that was happening. Second, I was experiencing more forgetfulness in my students. This was occurring on two levels: not remembering items like paper, pencils, and homework (This would have been a working memory problem or an attentional problem.) and also the lack of retrieval of information for assessment, especially paper and pencil tests.

How would you describe the relationship between memory and learning?

Simply put, without memory there is no learning. Many have explained these processes separately. Learning is making connections in the brain; memory is storing that information in a retrievable format. Learning and thus memory, alter behaviors, open doors to further learning, and make us who we are. Our brain is involved in everything we do, thus learning and memory physically change the brain.

Why do you think memory is such an important topic for teachers to know about?

Since our brains are involved in everything we do and everything that happens in school, I believe that it behooves all teachers to gain an understanding of how the brain works. Memory is the only evidence we have of learning. Whether students are assessed using authentic assessment, performance assessment, portfolios, or standardized paper and pencil tests, they rely on their memories to show what they have learned. Educators who understand how memory works can help all students to utilize the memory systems that work best for them. These same educators are sure to match the memory systems used in teaching to the memory systems needed for assessment. Recoding information into a student's own words, reflecting on the material, rehearsal, and review are steps in the memory process that make a big difference in student success. There is a seven step process described in my book, *How to Teach So Students Remember*, which helps all individuals store information in long term memory in a retrievable fashion.

What are some common misconceptions educators have about memory?

There are many common memory myths:

1. All memory is stored. The brain requires rehearsal and practice to remember. It is easier to forget than it is to remember.

2. When memories are recalled, they are recalled exactly as they were stored. In fact, each time we recall an event, it changes. Our brains have a way of "filling in the blanks" and often information is lost, embellished, or replaced with other, similar information.

3. "It's the student's job to remember. I just present the information." There are many scientifically based strategies that are known to improve memory and improve student achievement. If we are truly trying to help students learn and remember, we must guide them in utilizing the most practical and efficient approach to learning and memory.

4. Students will automatically remember what they have learned in my room and take it with them when they leave. This is an ideal scenario, but it just doesn't often happen. Transfer takes time, repetition, and true conceptual understanding of the material. The neuroscientists have told us that a person remembers better what they have learned when they are in the same location and under the same conditions under which they initially learned it.

What do you think teachers should impart to their students about memory skills?

I believe that students need to know about how their brain learns, how the different memory systems work, and about different memory strategies. Some students come to our classrooms with memory strategies that they have learned from others. But memory skills are similar to test-taking skills; they need to be reviewed each year.

Visual memory is becoming more important in this visual world of ours. There are more receptors in the brain for vision, and although students may have different learning styles, everyone needs to hone their visual skills.

What suggestions do you have for language learners who want to remember more vocabulary?

Emotion and meaning are the two most powerful ways to learn. Memorizing words and their meanings that are not attached to experiences or prior knowledge will not remain in long-term memory, if they ever get there at all. The scientifically based research suggests that vocabulary be taught explicitly. Students define a word, draw a picture of its meaning, find antonyms, synonyms, and write sentences. Then the word is taught in context. Review games are wonderful for increasing retention of the words. Debra Pickering suggests games like password in which one student offers information – definitions, synonyms, antonyms, etc to get another student to say the word. This is a powerful way to learn vocabulary as well as other concepts.

Can you share one of your favorite exercises from your workshops?

There are many fun exercises for memory. I like to take a list of unrelated words and make a story out of them, asking my participants to visualize the story as I tell it. Then they tell the story to another participant and check to see if they have all the words on the list. I then provide a new list of words for each of them to create a story, usually in pairs. The crazier the story, the easier it is to remember. The key is that if one can create a story out of unrelated words, using words that are related in a content area should be much easier and much more memorable.

What projects do you have coming up in the future?

My sixth book has just been released, *The Developing Brain – Birth through Age Eight*. I am excited about disseminating the information that combines neuroscience with cognitive psychology and child development. I am also in the process of working on a book on reading and the brain. As a language arts teacher for many of my years in the classroom, reading has always been a passion. I believe with the current brain research and memory research we can find ways to help struggling readers and to ensure the success of new readers.

———

Further reading

Books

Higbee, K. L. (1996). *Your memory.* New York: Marlowe.

Sprenger, M. (2007). *Memory 101 for educators.* Thousand Oaks, CA: Corwin Press.

Websites

Build Your Memory
http://www.buildyourmemory.com/

Exploratorium - The Memory Exhibition
http://www.exploratorium.edu/memory/index.html

3
Creativity

Creativity is an important skill that helps students develop imagination, produce ideas, and ultimately solve problems. Giving students opportunities to work creatively in class can be highly motivating and very enjoyable.

The activities in this chapter are designed to help students think freely, explore new ideas, and generate solutions to problems, along with activities that allow students to reflect on the creative process.

DEVELOPING STUDENT CREATIVITY

Teachers can do a number of things to develop students' creative skills. In an article titled "Generativity Theory", featured in the *Encyclopedia of Creativity*, Robert Epstein recommends 8 ways teachers can promote creativity in students:

- Encourage students to write down all new ideas.
- Present students with challenges such as problem solving, lateral thinking puzzles and riddles.
- Give students opportunities to expand their knowledge and learn new skills.
- Alter the environment (physical and social) on a regular basis.
- Put students in different groups and change the groups often. Also, have students switch between working on a problem individually and working together in a group.
- Provide plentiful resources for students to be creative.

- Give feedback at regular intervals. Acknowledge students' creative work.
- Set an example for the students, by demonstrating your own efforts to develop creatively.

THE BASICS OF BRAINSTORMING

Brainstorming is a well-known creative activity. In brainstorming, people work together in a small group to produce ideas.

Here are a few basic guidelines for brainstorming in class:

- Keep brainstorming groups small, around 3 to 7 students.

- Provide a relaxing atmosphere. You can play peaceful music or put pictures of nature on the wall.

- For problem solving activities, give the students a clear problem statement to work on. Problem statements can originate from topics in your coursebook, local issues or global issues. In addition, consider using issues that are relevant to your student's age group, school or community.

- Encourage students to generate a large number of ideas. It's best they don't settle on the first idea that comes to mind, but explore a broad range of ideas.

- Flights of fancy should be applauded. You should welcome all ideas, no matter how odd, nonsensical and wild they sound.

- Discourage any criticism of ideas. If anyone starts to criticize, assure them they can voice their concerns later. (Chapter Four - Critical Thinking includes several activities that can be used to help students choose among ideas generated in a brainstorming session.)

- Assign one student in each group to write down all the ideas.

Refer back to this list of guidelines when planning a brainstorming session, and also as you use the activities in this chapter.

If you plan to do brainstorming often, here are a few twists that can enrich your brainstorming sessions:

Time - Vary the amount of time you allow for brainstorming. Challenge them to brainstorm a fixed number of ideas in just a few minutes. Or let them brainstorm on their own over a weekend.

Place - Lead students outside the classroom to brainstorm in some novel location, if possible in your context.

Input - Provide a range of input (pictures, music, short readings, etc.) to stimulate their thinking.

Student-centeredness – Give students more control over the brain-storming. For example, students can write problem statements for each other or you can assign one student to lead a brainstorming activity.

Roles – In addition to electing one student to act as secretary, you can also create roles for other group members. A few possibilities are an encourager (gives encouragement to share ideas, no matter how out-landish), a questioner (asks questions, especially "why" and "what if" questions, to trigger more ideas), a supervisor (keeps the students on task and insists they use English as much as possible), and a summa-rizer (provides a quick recap of the group's ideas at the end of the ses-sion). For more about assigning student roles and their positive effect on the language learning process, read Chapter 7 of *Group Dynamics in the Language Classroom* by Zoltan Dörnyei and Tim Murphey.

Interaction between groups – Ask a group of students to write out a problem statement, then swap with another group. Or you can get a few students to switch groups in the middle of a brainstorming session.

Interaction with the outside world – Send students out into the hall-way to collect more ideas. You can also ask one member of each group to call a friend or family member on a cell phone.

Constraints – Set up some odd rules for the brainstorm. For example, each idea must be expressed in 7 words, or each idea must begin with a new letter of the alphabet (A, B, C…).

End product - Consider the different ways your students can present the results of their brainstorming, such as a poster, a short presentation, or a webpage.

PROBLEMS WITH BRAINSTORMING

In an article highly critical of the brainstorming process, Furnham (2000) indicates three problems that can make brainstorming sessions ineffective. These are:

1. Social loafing – participants produce fewer ideas than they would if they were working alone.

2. Evaluation apprehension – participants fail to let their ideas be heard out of fear of ridicule.

3. Production blocking – participants must wait for their turn to express their ideas, thus they either forget what they wanted to say or decide their ideas are not worth mentioning after hearing others' ideas.

Furnham gives a few pointers for improving the effectiveness of brain-storming. He suggests asking participants to list a specific number of ideas individually before the brainstorming session begins. The group should take breaks during the brainstorming session to do more individual idea production. Furthermore, he recommends breaking down the problem into smaller parts, as well as setting standards for the quality and quantity of the ideas.

TYPES OF BRAINSTORMING ACTIVITIES

There are three types of brainstorming activities well-suited to language learning: quick brainstorming, problem solving brainstorming, and mini-project brainstorming.

1. Quick brainstorming

In this type of activity, students make a list of as many items as they can in a short period of time. This can be done at the beginning of class, to ease students back into speaking English after speaking their native language for many hours outside of class. It can be a good way to introduce the topic of a lesson.

Here are a few examples:

- Draw a small blob on the board. What is it? (an amoeba, a lake, an island, etc.)
- Words that start with the letter B
- Words that rhyme with cat
- Fill in the blank (ex. He was surprised to see a _____ in his chair.)
- Things that make a loud noise
- Things that are expensive
- People you admire
- Bands you think are overrated
- Things you have in common with the people in your group
- Places you want to visit
- Things you can buy with less than $5
- Collocations of "time"
- Words that are four syllables long
- Different ways to say goodbye
- Familiar advertising slogans

Cullen (1998) has many more suggestions for this type of brainstorming.

2. Problem solving brainstorming

The teacher (or class) comes up with a problem and students brainstorm several solutions. The problem can be summarized in a problem statement (a sentence or a question that describes the problem). Another approach is to present a problem in a dramatic paragraph.

A few examples:

- How can we make our classroom a more pleasant place to learn in?
- How can we take a class trip without spending a lot of money?
- How can we improve our study habits?
- How can we reduce littering around our school?
- How can we improve our English pronunciation?
- How can we maximize the use of our learning time in class?

- Lately you have noticed that your father spends a lot of time in front of the computer. You wish he would spend more time with the rest of the family. Think of some ways to improve this situation.

- You and your classmates have a problem with your French teacher. She speaks too fast, and often speaks to the class with her face turned towards the board. She's a strict teacher, so you don't want to offend her. Think of several solutions.

- For the past month, your sister has been down in the dumps. She looks sad all the time, and never seems to show much interest in anything. Think of a few things you can do to cheer her up.

- The food at your school's cafeteria is unhealthy and unappetizing. All the students agree that the cafeteria's food is awful. Yet, it's the most convenient place to have lunch. Think of one or two ways to improve this situation.

- A small business has just given your teacher 683 small cardboard boxes. They fit in the palm of your hand, and are completely blank on all sides. Devise a number of different ways your class could use these boxes.

- One of your classmates is constantly saying bad things about the other students to the teacher. Many of the students are unhappy with this and don't trust him. Think of a bunch of things you can do to solve this problem.

- Your cousin is planning to start at your school next year. Think of some different ways you could introduce her to the school.

Seek out Donald J. Treffinger's book *Practice Problems for Creative Problem Solving* for more problem statements.

3. Mini-project brainstorming

The teacher presents something to be designed or created, and students work in groups to produce it. These can be highly motivating, as students can see a finished product in the end. They can be carried out in 30 minutes, an hour, or extended into longer projects that take several weeks to complete. For a longer more extensive activity, teachers can start by introducing useful vocabulary and showing examples. Next, the project can go through several drafts with input from the teacher as well as peer review. (For more information about doing projects in the language classroom, consult Diana L. Fried-Booth's book, *Project Work*.)

A few examples:

- Design a new gadget
- Create a new reality TV show
- Produce a new and improved coursebook cover
- Make a new soft drink
- Think of a new game for learning English
- Design a new school uniform
- Make your own comic strip
- Write a recipe for the ideal snack

- Create a new country
- Invent a new language

(Chapter Five contains two examples of mini-project brainstorming, 5.8 Attribute listing and 5.9 Creating the ultimate.)

ENCOURAGING STUDENTS TO SPEAK IN ENGLISH

Brainstorming is a good way to help students develop fluency in English. Therefore, it's extremely important that students use English while brainstorming. Students may revert back to their first language for a multitude of reasons: they feel uncomfortable speaking English, they don't think it's "cool" to use English, or simply because it's so much easier to do the activity in their own language.

For classes that are reluctant to speak English, here are a few strategies to try out. First of all, address the issue in the first class. Let students know the importance of using only English, and that you expect them to use English most of the time. Praise students when you hear them using English in class. Insist that students communicate with you in English. Give students plenty of listening activities, so they become accustomed to hearing English.

You can also introduce some small changes into group work. One option is to use rewards. During an activity, you can give a group one point each time they use their first language, and award a prize to the group with the lowest number of points. Another idea is to have them do an activity twice, the first time in their native language, and the second time in English. Alternatively, you can ask one student in each group to keep track of how much English the group speaks, and give you a report at the end of the activity.

———

3.1 Quick solutions

Aims – Language of making suggestions, speaking
Time - 15 minutes
Preparation – Think up some sentences for the sentence starters in step 1.

1. Provide students with these sentence starters:

"I've got an idea. You could _____."
"I think you should _____."
"I suggest _____."
"One possible solution is _____."

Give them a few examples of how each could be used.

2. Arrange chairs in a circle, and include one extra chair.

3. Tell students about a problem you are facing and ask them to think of a solution. Instruct them to remain silent for a couple of minutes.

4. Tell the class if someone wants to share a solution, he or she should go sit in the empty chair to speak. The next student who wants to describe a solution must go and sit in the seat vacated by the previous student. Continue 5 or 6 times.

5. Now give students a few minutes to think of a problem in their own lives. It could be a problem with a friend or family member, or a goal they want to reach, such as losing weight or saving money to buy something. Call on a student to describe his or her problem. Repeat step 4.

3.2 Speed date for speedy solutions

Aims – Fluency practice, speaking, listening, writing, reading
Time - 20 minutes
Preparation – None

1. Ask students to think about a problem they are currently facing. Ask them to sit silently and think about how they would explain this problem to another person.

2. Now arrange chairs where you have two rows of seats facing each other.

3. Tell students they are going to share solutions using a "speed-date" format. If your students don't know what speed-dating is, tell them it's a dating activity where singles can meet a lot of different people in a short period of time. Emphasize that they will not be looking for romance, but seeking solutions for their problems.

4. Here's the format: During each interaction, students need to decide who wants to seek advice and who wants to offer advice. The student with the problem must share his problem and the other student must give some advice. Each turn will last only 2 minutes, and then they will switch partners. They do this by having each student in one row move down, while the students in the other row remain where they are. The student on the end of the moving row must move to the empty seat on the other side of the line.

5. When they have done this six or seven times, ask students to move back to where they were sitting and write a short paragraph about some advice they gave or received.

Read out these questions to get them started:

Did you get any useful advice?
Who gave you the best advice?
How did you feel about giving advice?

Do you plan to make any changes based on what you heard? What steps could you take to follow someone's advice?

6. Get students to put their paragraphs up on the walls for everyone to read.

Variation: Instead of having each interaction last 2 minutes, you can make the first one 3.5 minutes, the second 3 minutes, the third 2.5 minutes, the fourth 2 minutes, the fifth 1.5 minutes, and the sixth 1 minute.

3.3 Jigsaw problem solving

Aims – Listening, writing, reading, discussion, speaking, listening
Time - 45 minutes
Preparation – Prepare copies of the paragraph in step 1.

1. Tell students you are going to give them a dictogloss (use the following paragraph or compose your own). You want them to listen, but not write anything down as you read the following paragraph to them:

> "Imagine it's your first day here. You have transferred to this school in the middle of the school year. You have moved here from a small town far away, and you don't know anyone here. You look around the classroom and you don't feel welcome. You are very nervous. What can you do to get more settled into this new place?"

Read out the paragraph again, and again tell them not to take notes. Finally, say you are going to read it one more time, and you want them to write down a few keywords from the paragraph. Read the paragraph once more.

2. Get students working in pairs. They need to reconstruct the paragraph from their notes. After a few minutes, choose 4 pairs to write their version of the paragraph on the board. Pass out copies of the paragraph, and ask each pair to compare their version with the original.

3. Divide students into 4 groups. The first group will try to think of the most unusual, outlandish solutions they can and write them down. The second group will come up with practical solutions. The third group will close their eyes and imagine solutions. The fourth group will look around the classroom for anything that suggests a solution to the problem. Emphasize that each group needs to write down all of their solutions.

4. After 15 minutes, create new groups, with each group containing one member of the four previous groups. Tell them to take turns describing the work they did in their first group and the solutions they came up with.

5. Finally, ask each group to vote on their best ideas. They should write their top 3 solutions on the board.

3.4 Incubation period

Aims – Speaking, listening, writing, reading, revising, using linkers
Time – 2 class periods (1st class period - 30 minutes, 2nd class period - 30 minutes)
Preparation – Bring envelopes to class

1. Ask students to work in groups of three. Their task is to write a ten word summary of a problem or a goal one of them is currently concerned with. After a few minutes, let a representative from each group write the summary on the board.

2. Tell students to come to the board and take a vote on which problem they want to explore together as a class. They should put a check next to any problem they want to work on. The problem that garners the most checks is the one that will be used for this activity.

3. Give each student a piece of paper and an envelope. Tell them to write a solution to the problem in 3 sentences, then seal it in the envelope. Ask students to write their names on the envelopes.

4. Collect the envelopes and tell students they will continue the activity in a later class.

5. Several weeks later, hand out the envelopes, and make sure that everyone gets another student's envelope. Tell them to read the solution, and then expand it into a paragraph of 10 sentences. Stress that they need to develop the ideas on the page and expand on the three sentences. Encourage use of linkers, such as "first of all", "therefore", "however", "furthermore", and "finally".

6. When they are finished writing, put students in pairs to read each other their paragraphs, and suggest improvements.

7. For homework, assign students to write a new draft of the paragraph.

3.5 Inside - outside

Aims – Reading, writing, listening, speaking, detecting errors
Time – 1 hour
Preparation - Think of a problem you want students to discuss. Prepare copies of two one-page articles, one about the problem, and another on a subject completely unrelated to the problem. Make enough copies for half the class.

1. Arrange chairs in two circles, one inside the other. Make sure there is plenty of room to move between both circles.

2. Write your problem statement on the board. Also write 10 – 12 keywords that relate to your problem statement in the area around the problem statement. Ask students to come to the board and write a few words in their own language about the problem.

3. Now divide the class into two groups. One group will sit in the inner circle, and the other group will sit in the outer circle. Tell students in the inner circle to discuss the problem and think of some solutions, while students in the outer circle will read the article that is unrelated to the problem. After 5 minutes, tell each group to switch places and tasks for another 5 minutes.

4. Repeat step 3, but now swap the articles.

5. Give students 10 minutes to write down all the solutions that came up.

6. Collect their papers. Announce that you are going to give a dictation of their sentences. Tell them that you will read 6 correct sentences and 4 sentences with errors in them. They need to write them down and correct the errors. Read out 10 of their sentences, avoiding repetition of any solutions.

7. After the dictation, choose students to write the sentences on the board. Point out any errors. Finally, invite students to comment on the solutions.

3.6 Role playing for solutions

Aims – Listening, speaking, word order, reading, writing
Time - 45 minutes
Preparation – None

1. Read out the following paragraph to the class:

"Imagine one day one of your classmates accuses you of stealing his laptop computer. It's a very expensive model. Just yesterday, he was a good friend, but now he regards you with suspicion and hostility. You have told him several times that he's making a mistake, but he refuses to believe you. You're worried that he is going to talk to your teacher or school administration and get you in trouble. How can you deal with this situation?"

Read it again. Ask one or two students to repeat the main points of the paragraph.

2. Put students in groups of 4 to create a role play about the problem you mentioned. Emphasize that you do not want them to mention a solution in the role play, only the problem. Ask them to rehearse the role play several times in their group and tell you when they are ready.

3. Have each group perform their role play for the class. After each role play, get the other groups to ask the group some questions about how they presented the problem.

4. Now put students into pairs. Have each pair produce a list of 10 solutions. When they are finished, each pair should write one solution on the board, but with the words in the wrong order.

5. Call on volunteers to unscramble the sentences on the board, writing the correct version under the scrambled sentence. Ask the original authors to check. Once the students have the correct order, they can erase the scrambled sentence.

6. Ask several students to tell you which solution they prefer and why.

3.7 Courtesan, warrior and observer

Aims – Reading, listening, writing, speaking, asking and answering questions
Time - 45 minutes
Preparation – Make one copy of each of the texts below. Prepare index cards with the numbers 1, 2, and 3. There should be one card for every student in the class.

1. Hand out the following texts to three students and ask them to go to the board:

> (1) I am a very submissive person. I seek one person who under-stands me and can give me the intimacy that I need. I don't like being the center of attention. I'm very sensitive to criticism. My big-gest fear is that my friends will abandon me.

> (2) I'm an achiever. I'm extremely competitive, and I like to have power over others. I prefer competition over cooperation. I'm a sore loser, and I can get very rude if someone bothers me. I crave the attention and admiration of others.

> (3) I'm very detached from things. I enjoy having privacy and isola-tion. I like to do most things alone. I like to discover things by my-self, and I don't rely on information from other people. I aim to be a self-sufficient, independent person.

Then choose three more students to go to the board. Give each of the writers a different colored piece of chalk. The students with the texts must each stand behind a different student and read out the text while the other student writes it up on the board. The students with the texts must read them aloud, and not show them to the writers.

2. Next, randomly distribute a card with a number on it to each student. Students should read over the text that corresponds with the number

they have been given. Then they must create a character based on the description. They need to imagine and write down at least 20 details about this person, such as hair color, mannerisms, occupation, favorite book, or anything else the student wants to include.

3. After about 10 minutes of writing and thinking, invite a student to come to the front and role play his or her character. Encourage him or her to get into character. The students can ask him or her questions. Repeat this step a few times with different students.

4. Call on one student to read out this problem statement (or make your own problem statement for this activity):

The Smith family is in a major conflict over which TV program to watch on Saturday night at 7 p.m. All of their favorite shows are on at the same time! Mr. Smith wants to watch "14 Hours", the TV newsmagazine. He says it's educational and will help the family learn more about the world. Mrs. Smith wants to watch "Family Portrait", which is a situation comedy. She says it's very funny and promotes family values. Meanwhile, Tom, their son (a high school student), wants to watch "Gun Alley", an action series. He says it's very exciting, and describes the life of a policeman. Now no one is talking to each other, and it's getting close to Saturday night.

5. Invite a student with a #1 card to come up and give his or her opinion about the problem, as well as some solutions. Do the same with #2 and #3.

6. Finally, put students into groups so that there is a #1, #2, and #3 in every group. Get groups to discuss a number of solutions. Finally, each group must agree on one solution and write it up on the board.

Acknowledgement: I read about Karen Horney's concepts of the Courtesan, the Warrior and the Observer in Malcolm Godwin's fascinating book *Who Are You?: 101 Ways of Seeing Yourself*.

3.8 Sleep on it

Aims – Writing, discussion
Time - 2 class periods (1st class period - 15 minutes, 2nd class period - 10 minutes)
Materials – Bring a lot of index cards to class.

1. Write this problem statement on the board (you can also substitute one of your own):

A classmate of yours, John, is madly in love with Becky, another class-mate. He often talks about how beautiful she is, and how he wishes they were a couple. However, Becky is not interested. She ignores John's attempts to woo her, and has made it clear to everyone she's not looking for a boyfriend.

To make it more interesting, leave out a few letters in some of the words. Invite students to come to the board and fill in the missing letters.

2. Ask students to think of a sentence that summarizes this issue using different words. Emphasize that you are NOT asking them to find a so-lution, but alternative ways of describing the problem.

3. Tell students to write their sentences up on the board around the problem statement.

4. At the end of class, give each student a few index cards. Tell them to place the cards along with a pen next their beds. Before bedtime, you want them to think about the problem for 2 or 3 minutes, then stop and go to sleep. The following day, they need to write down any solutions that come to mind when they wake up.

5. In the next class period, invite students to share their experiences in pairs. Then call on students to talk about it. How many students wrote something down? Did anyone think of something really interesting?

3.9 Whose solution?

Aims – Writing, listening, guessing
Time - 30 minutes
Preparation – Bring a set of index cards to class.

1. Give students this problem statement (or use one of your own):

Imagine there is a student in your class you really can't stand. He sits in the back, makes insulting comments about the other students, and frequently interrupts the teacher with rude remarks. What would you do about this student?

2. Tell each student they must write their solution to the problem in exactly 25 words. Students should not write their names on the cards. Ask students to hand in the cards when they are finished.

3. When you have collected all the cards, read one of them out. Can the students guess who wrote it? Allow a few guesses, then let the author identify him or herself. Then call on a few students to ask the author a question. Repeat the process with 3 or 4 other cards.

Variation: After finishing step 2, give each student a different student's card and tell them to stand up and mingle. Each student must try to find the person who wrote the solution on their card by asking questions such as "Did your solution involve talking to the teacher?" or "Did you use a lot of adjectives in your solution?"

3.10 Xerox problem solving process

Aims – Reading, ordering, speaking, writing, using detail in writing
Time – 1 hour
Preparation – Bring many index cards to class.

1. Ask your students to close their eyes and think of a time when they solved a problem. Tell them to identify some of the steps they took to solve it.

2. Now put students in pairs to compare their steps. While they are discussing, put this up on the board:

The Xerox Problem Solving Process

Implement the solution
Analyze the problem
Evaluate the solution
Identify the problem
Select and plan the solution
Generate potential solutions

Tell students that this is a problem solving process known as the Xerox Problem Solving Process. However, you have mixed up the order of the steps. Get students to work in pairs to put the steps into their proper order.

Here are the steps in the correct order:

1-Identify the problem
2-Analyze the problem
3-Generate potential solutions
4-Select and plan the solution
5-Implement the solution
6-Evaluate the solution

3. Read out the 6 steps and explain them to the students. In the first step, you decide what problem you want to work on. In the second step, you explore what is causing the problem. In the third step, you brainstorm some solutions. In the fourth step, you choose the best solution and create an action plan. In the fifth step, you put the solution into practice. In the sixth step, you assess how well you did. Call on several students to tell you if there are any similarities between the steps of the Xerox Problem Solving Process and the steps they wrote down.

4. Invite a few students to tell you a few concrete actions they could take to finish each step. (For example, in the first step, a person could spend an afternoon at a coffee shop, jotting down notes about things that frustrate them on a paper napkin.)

5. Give each student an index card and tell them to write down the name of a profession, such as a CEO, a waitress, or a farmer.

6. Collect the cards, then give each student a card which is not their own.

7. Tell students to look at the card you gave them. They should imagine a person with this profession is facing a problem and needs to solve it using the Xerox Problem Solving Process.

8. Give each student six index cards. Tell them to write about two or three sentences about a different step on each card. They should not number the cards or write the name of the steps on any of them. Emphasize that you want them to use a lot of sensory detail in their essays.

9. When they're finished writing, put them into pairs. They should mix up their cards and hand them to their partner. Their partner's task is to read the cards, and attempt to put them back into order. Also, ask students to explain why they chose the order they did.

10. Finally, ask a few students to tell the class about their partner's problem solving story.

Acknowledgement: I learned about the Xerox Problem Solving Process in John Middleton's book, Upgrade Your Brain.

3.11 Global brainstorming

Aims – Speaking, listening, reading, writing
Time – 1 hour
Preparation – None

1. Read out the following text to the class:

The world leaders need your help! Leaders of all countries in the world have gathered together in order to finally solve all the major problems facing planet Earth. However, they would like your input. First you must decide what the most serious problems are. Then you need to rank them in order of importance, and choose the most important one. Finally, you will discuss some solutions.

2. Ask students to call out the main problems. These might include global warming, terrorism, as well as others. Write the problems on the board.

3. Next, put them in groups of five or six students. Tell them to work together and rank the problems. Which problems are the most important?

4. Call on each group to tell you their top 3 problems. On the board, circle the ones that are mentioned.

5. Next, ask the class to decide on which problem should get priority. This will be the topic of the rest of the lesson. Erase the board.

6. Write the following questions across the board at the top:

What are the origins of this problem?
What are the consequences (good and bad) of having this problem solved?
What are the consequences of not solving the problem?
Who is directly involved in this problem?

Draw vertical lines to separate the board into four areas, one for each question.

7. Divide students into four groups, and assign each group to a question on the board. Ask each group to write several answers under their question.

8. After 5 minutes, tell students to change places. Do this 2 more times, so that everyone has a chance to answer all the questions.

9. Now give students some time to read and add additional comments.

10. Tell the class to return to their seats and write a short paragraph describing one solution to the problem.

11. Call on several students to read out their paragraphs, and ask them questions.

3.12 Killer phrases

Aims – Speaking, listening, writing, language of discouragement, language of encouragement
Time - 15 minutes
Preparation – None

1. Introduce your class to the concept of killer phrases, things people say which stifle creativity during brainstorming. Write some of the following on the board:

It'll never work.
That's impossible.
That's a bad idea.
That's ridiculous.
That's the worst idea I've ever heard.
What a bunch of nonsense!

Ask a student how he or she would feel if he or she suggested an idea and heard one of these killer phrases.

2. Put students into pairs. Ask them to make a list of 3 more killer phrases.

3. Call on each pair to read out their deadliest killer phrase. Write them on the board, correcting any errors.

4. Now put students in groups of 5. Remind students that one important aspect of brainstorming is to encourage people to create many new ideas and resist the urge to criticize. Ask each group to produce a list of 3 phrases that support creativity, such as "That's a terrific idea!"

5. Erase the killer phrases from the board. Ask each group to put their best phrase on the board.

6. Read out the phrases on the board, and ask the class to repeat them with you.

7. Put students in groups to brainstorm and have them use some of the phrases on the board.

3.13 Brainstorming race

Aims – Speaking, writing, reading, discussion
Time - 30 minutes
Preparation – Think of 5 problem statements that could generate a large number of solutions. Create a different handout for each problem statement. Put a problem statement at the top of each sheet, and put the numbers 1 to 10 on the left side of the page. Put each handout in an envelope, seal it and hide each one somewhere in the classroom before students arrive. Prepare a small prize.

1. At the start of class, put students into 5 groups. Tell each group they need to find an envelope hidden somewhere in the classroom. Each envelope contains a problem statement. When a group finds it, they must sit down and think of 10 solutions to the problem. They will write these solutions on the handout, and tell you when they are finished. The first group to finish gets a prize.

2. Circulate and make sure students understand the activity. If a group finishes before the others, ask them to add 3 more solutions to their handout. Also, ask them to check over their paper for errors.

3. When all groups are finished, ask students to put their handouts up on the board. Award a prize to the group who finished first.

4. Bring students up to the board to look over the handouts. Ask each group to add one more solution to the other groups' handouts.

5. Finally, look over the sheets and read out some of the solutions. Ask the groups some questions about their solutions.

3.14 Brainstorming challenge

Aims – Fluency practice, speaking, error correction
Time - 30 minutes
Preparation – Purchase a small prize for the winning team (optional)

1. Assign a brainstorming task. Divide the class into two groups and give them one of the following challenges:

- each team must create as many ideas as possible in 7 minutes. The team with the most ideas wins the game.
- a team must create 10 ideas to win the game (no time limit).
- each team must create as many ideas as possible in 5 minutes, and the team with the most ideas that are not on the other team's list wins the game.
- each team must create a problem for the other team to solve, 2 students (not on either team) act as judges and must decide which team came up with the best solutions.

2. As students work on the challenge, circulate and write down any errors you hear.

3. Announce a winner and award a prize. Also, ask the winning group to read out their ideas. Again, copy any errors you hear.

4. During a break, make a list of five sentences that contain errors, both from the student's spoken language during the brainstorming task, and also from their lists of ideas. Next to each sentence, write the correct form of the sentence.

5. Tell students you want to give them a dictation. Explain that you will read out two versions of some of their sentences (one correct version and one incorrect version). They need to write down the correct version. Read out the sentences. (Mix the order for each one, so that

you sometimes read the correct version first, and sometimes read the incorrect version first.)

6. Put students in pairs to compare their answers.

7. Call on students to write the 5 sentences on the board. Make corrections if necessary.

3.15 Idea-friendly times

Aims – Guessing, reading, listening, writing, discussion
Time - 20 minutes
Preparation – Bring a copy of the list to class.

1. Ask the class when and where they get creative ideas. Wait for a few answers.

2. Tell them that you have a list of the top ten "idea-friendly" times. Based on the informal research of a creativity expert, Chic Thompson, this list contains the most common situations where people come up with new ideas. Give students a few minutes to guess 3 items on the list.

3. When they are ready, dictate the list to them.

Idea-Friendly Times

10. While performing manual labor.
 9. While listening to a church sermon.
 8. On waking up in the middle of the night.
 7. While exercising.
 6. During leisure reading.
 5. During a boring meeting.
 4. While falling asleep or waking up.
 3. While commuting to work.
 2. While showering or shaving.
 1. While sitting on the toilet.

source: *What a Great Idea! 2.0* by Chic Thompson (Sterling)

---

4. Did they guess any of the items correctly? Ask students to compare their answers with a partner.

5. Ask students to check each activity that they usually do. Also, ask several students if they can think of any other idea-friendly times that are not mentioned on the list.

6. For homework, ask students to pay attention the next time they are in one of these situations, and write down any ideas that come to them.

3.16 E-mail competition

Aims – Reading, writing, listening, speaking, revising, error correction
Time – A few minutes in several class periods
Preparation – Make sure that all students have e-mail accounts and you have a list of all their e-mail addresses. This activity works best with students who use e-mail on a regular basis.

1. In class, tell students that you want to invite them to participate in a competition that will give them an opportunity to exercise their creativity. Remind them to check their e-mails during the next day or two for details about the competition.

2. After class, send out an e-mail to all students with a problem state-ment that could have a wide variety of solutions. Students must send you their 3 best ideas before a stated deadline.

3. When the deadline arrives, make a list of all the ideas, eliminating any duplicates, and correcting errors. Give each idea a number. Also, copy all sentences containing errors onto another page.

4. During the next class period, thank students for their enthusias-tic participation. Tell them to check their e-mail during the next few days, as you are going to send them a list of all the ideas you received. Also, in the same class period, write a few of their sentences which originally contained errors on the board. Choose several students to go to the board to correct the errors.

5. After class, send the complete error-free list of ideas out to students by e-mail. Praise their innovative ideas, and tell them to vote for the 3 best ideas, ranking them in order (1^{stt}, 2nd, 3rd). As in the previous stage, give them a deadline.

6. Once the deadline arrives, you must tally up the votes. Each time an idea gets voted #1, give it 3 points. #2 gets 2 points, and #3 gets 1 point. Add up the total number of points for each idea. Create another

list, ranking the ideas in order of points. However, DO NOT send out this list.

7. In class, remind students of the ongoing competition. Tell them you have counted all of the votes and declared a winner. Stress that they need to check their e-mail for more information.

8. Send an e-mail to students telling them you have calculated the votes, but you are not going to tell them the scores. Instead, challenge them to guess which 3 ideas got the highest scores. Send them the same list as in step 5, and ask them to guess the 3 ideas they think got the most points. They must send you the list before a deadline.

9. Finally, in class, present a prize to the student (or students) whose guess was the closest. Also give 3 more prizes to the students whose ideas were in the top three.

10. Next dictate the 3 winning ideas to the class. Ask them to rewrite each idea twice. In each case, they should use different vocabulary and grammar to express roughly the same ideas. Give them a few minutes to write.

11. Call a student's name. Ask that student to choose an idea and call on another student to read out an alternate version. Repeat several times, until the class has read out several versions of each idea.

Acknowledgement: This idea is based on the "C3PO Game" in the book *Design Your Own Games and Activities* by Sivasailam (Thiagi) Thiagarajan with Raja Thiagarajan.

3.17 Borrowed solutions

Aims - Writing, reading, discussion
Time - 30 minutes
Preparation - Bring lots of index cards to class.

1. Ask students to write about a problem they're concerned about. It could be a personal, national or global issue. Tell them to each write about half a page on their problem.

2. Now give each student 5 index cards. On each card, the students should write 1 solution to the problem they just wrote about.

3. Collect the cards, shuffle them and give each student a card. Ask them to tell you if they get their own cards, so you can give them different ones.

4. Tell students to use the unrelated solution on their card as a springboard for a new solution to their problems. They need to write three new solutions that are in some way suggested by the other student's solution.

5. Put the rest of the cards on your desk, and invite students to come up and draw another card to repeat step 4.

6. Put them in groups of three to discuss their problems and solutions.

3.18 Reading - "10 Ways to Boost Your Creativity"

Aims – Listening, writing, guessing content of a text, learning new vocabulary, writing, reading
Time - 2 class periods (1st class period - 1 hour, 2nd class period - 30 minutes)
Preparation – Prepare copies of the article.

1. Choose a student to come up to the board. Read out the following 3 words, and ask the student to write them in different places on the board: quiet, talk, enjoy.

2. Then ask the student to get someone else to take over and write up these words: read, tourist, script.

3. Get one more student to write up these words: routine, what if, childlike.

4. Tell the class that they are about to read an article titled "10 Ways to Boost Your Creativity," and the words on the board are clues to the content of the article. Put them in pairs and ask them to guess 3 of the 10 ways to boost creativity mentioned in the article.

5. Ask each pair to read out one of their guesses.

6. Preteach the following vocabulary: birthright, facilitate, resurrect, enhance, feasible, assumptions, storyboard, viewpoint

7. Pass out copies of the article, and ask students to check if the article includes any of their ideas.

8. Ask several students if the article mentioned the ways they discussed in step 4.

9. Erase the board, and invite students to write on the board any of the ways they talked about that are not in the article, but they think the class would like to know about.

10. Assign students to read the article again, and choose one tip they would like to follow for the next week.

11. Next week, in class, ask students to write a short paragraph about the tip they used, and what they experienced. Later, choose a few students to read their paragraphs to the class.

Note: This article was written by Julie Plenty, a Personal and Business coach. Visit her blog at: http://www.allowingabundance.blogspot. com/

------

10 Ways to Boost Your Creativity
By Julie Plenty

Creativity is your birthright — but can often be hidden in the everyday. To facilitate your personal development and self growth, here are some creativity tips you can use to resurrect, refresh and enhance your creative faculties.

1. Look after yourself.
Sleep well/Eat well/meditate/do what you enjoy and do it more often (if it is life enhancing!). Creativity is reduced when your senses are dulled.

2. Do something different.
We do so much on auto — the route we take to work, newspaper we read, TV programmes we routinely watch. Vary one element of your regular routine for a while. If feasible, take a different route to work, read a different newspaper (especially one you would never read!).

3. Be curious about your world around you.
It always amazes me when people don't see what's around them. See the area you live/work in as a tourist would. How would you explore it if you were a tourist?

4. Read a book on something you previously had no interest in.
...and see if you can create interest whilst reading it. It is my belief that no topic is boring or uninteresting if it is enthusiastically and creatively presented. You know what you like — or you like what you know?

5. Do something childlike once in a while.
...and you don't have to have the children there as an "excuse" to do it. Sit and play on swings/draw/paint "silly" pictures — have fun. Children are incredibly creative and as adults we could learn a lot about how they view the world.

6. Create/prepare quiet time for yourself every day.
Not to do anything (unless it relaxes you), but just to clear and refresh your mind. We are human beings, not doings. There are times when our crowded schedule and minds don't allow space and time for the creative to be welcomed in. Einstein liked to go sailing in the afternoons after working in the morning. Okay, most of us don't have this opportunity, but you get the point.

7. Ask "what if" questions.
Just for fun and see where the answers take you. What if that building could talk, what would it say, what stories would it tell?

8. We often make assumptions.
...about the people we work with (especially if we don't like them!) Try treating someone you don't particularly like at work as if you liked them (yeah I know...). What would you say, how would you act towards them?

9. Write and storyboard your life.
...as if it were a script you had to sell to a film company.

10. Talk to people you routinely ignore or dismiss.
Imagine their lives from their point of view, they often have viewpoints which you may never have considered before and carry a small notebook with you to jot down new ideas / sensations / feelings as they come to mind.

Do one, some or all of these and you'll soon notice a rise in your creativity, personal development and self growth.

http://www.creativity-portal.com/bc/other/boost.creativity.shtml

---

For the Teacher

This section contains an interview with Dr. Alane Starko. Here she shares her professional experience and relays some practical information on fostering creativity in the classroom.

An Interview with Dr. Alane Starko

Dr. Alane Starko is a professor in the Department of Teacher Education at Eastern Michigan University. She is a former head of that department and also a former elementary school teacher, teacher of the gifted, and member of the Board of Directors of the National Association for Gifted Children. She is the author of *Creativity in the Classroom: Schools of Curious Delight* and several other books on teacher preparation and teaching research to young people. She lives in Ann Arbor, Michigan with her husband and four creative cats.

How did you initially get interested in the subject of creativity?

I've been interested in creative activities on a personal level for as long as I can remember. As a little girl I loved creating spaceship controls in the closet and impromptu musical productions on the playground. So, from one perspective this has been a long-term interest. But my professional interest came much later. I was first exposed to academic study of creativity as a doctoral student at the University of Connecticut, and I was immediately hooked.

What is the relationship between creativity and learning?

In one sense, it depends on the definition of creativity you are using. Some theorists would suggest that each time we develop a new idea—or even a new sentence—we are using the same cognitive processes as are used in creativity. Other definitions of creativity are more constrained.

From a teacher's perspective, I think the most important thing to understand is that the activities and habits-of-mind that facilitate creativity, facilitate learning as well. For example, when students examine ideas from multiple perspectives, generate questions and problems, and express ideas in multiple ways, those processes build understanding and encourage creativity at the same time.

Why do you think teachers should know more about creativity?

Most teachers I know want to understand their students and help them learn. We understand that teaching strategies that encourage creativity help students learn. If we learn those strategies and use them, we are likely to be more successful in our teaching. Strategies that encourage the intrinsic motivation that is linked to creativity also can help motivate students in learning needed content.

In addition, understanding more about creativity can help us understand our students better. Creative thinking may lead students to approach ideas and assignments in unusual ways. Understanding more about creativity can help us see those responses as an indication of potential instead of a problem. If we want students to develop the creative thinking skills that I believe are essential for our rapidly changing world, we must be willing—and even anxious—to work with student responses that aren't what we expected, and go in directions we had not planned. This can be challenging for teachers, but I think it makes the job more fun.

What are some common misconceptions people have about creativity?

I think that many people view creativity as a "frill," particularly in schools. They envision creativity as almost synonymous with play, assuming creative activities are always enjoyable "extras," separate from the real serious work of the rest of the world. This vision of creative and flexible ideas as less valuable—and perhaps even less virtuous—than traditional learning and work can lead us to make terribly foolish decisions. To the degree that we try to reduce school to rote inflexible learning, we won't teach the content very well—while simultaneously eliminating the kind of flexible thinking that is absolutely necessary for our rapidly changing world.

What do you think teachers should impart to their students about creativity?

It is hard for me to separate things I'd hope students would understand about creativity from things they need to understand about learning. These would include things like the following:

- The world is a fascinating place and people do interesting things. The more we understand them, the more interesting they are. We should be open to the wonder of people and things around us. Looking at things through other people's eyes helps their actions make sense.

- Thinking people ask questions and have more interesting lives. The best questions don't have answers in the back of the book.

- Having lots of ideas is good. Your first idea is practically never your best idea (this became something of a mantra for my elementary school students!) Viewing things in different ways can be interesting and lead to new ideas.

- Having lots of ideas means sometimes you make mistakes. Every mistake teaches us something.

- Important ideas and important work take time and effort. Smart creative people have to work hard to do interesting things.

How would teachers help students understand these things?

I like to think about three keys to a "creativity-friendly" classroom. These are:

1. Directly teaching skills and attitudes associated with creativity.

2. Teaching the problem-finding and problem-solving techniques of the disciplines. This means teaching the "how" of our subjects and not just the "what."

3. Working toward a classroom atmosphere that supports intrinsic motivation and creativity.

Can you share one of your favorite exercises from your classes?

My favorite activity in my adult classes on creativity is the invention assignment. Each student must identify a problem in the real world and invent something to solve it. The invention must really work; it can't just be imaginary. I like this assignment because even though students are very worried about it, I've never had a student who didn't succeed. When they arrive at class with their completed inventions, students are almost always happy and proud. It is fun to see them conquer something they don't think they can manage and come out successful.

What new additions will be included in the next edition of your book, *Creativity in the Classroom*?

Of course the first task of any new edition is to update the research and theories to reflect the more current thoughts. In terms of new content, I am very interested in how concepts of creativity vary cross-culturally, so there is more information about that throughout the next edition. I'm also working on more examples of content-specific lessons, particularly for older students. I'm reorganizing the text into ten chapters instead of eight, cutting some of the longer chapters in half and rearranging others so that individual chapters aren't so long. Some professors prefer to assign a whole chapter at a time, and this should help that. And, of course, the next edition isn't completed yet, so there may be new surprises yet to come!

Further reading

Books

Starko, A. (2009). *Creativity in the classroom*. New York: Routledge.

Michalko, M. (2001). *Cracking creativity*. Berkeley, CA: Ten Speed Press.

Websites

Creativity Web
http://members.optusnet.com.au/~charles57/Creative/

Dr. Leslie Wilson – Creativity Index
http://www.uwsp.edu/education/lwilson/creativ/index.htm

4
Critical Thinking

While creativity involves the production of new ideas, critical thinking is more concerned with judging and evaluating ideas. The critical thinking movement began in the early 70's. Most courses in critical thinking centered on the study of logic and analyzing the structure of arguments. In the mid 80's, critical thinking courses became more diverse, and emphasized the application of critical thinking theory. Currently, a search for books on critical thinking on the Amazon.com website gives over 43,000 results, including not only introductory textbooks on critical thinking, but also books on critical thinking in nursing and psychology.

A critical thinking approach can add a new dimension to language learning. Day (2003) identifies three areas of critical thinking that he emphasizes when teaching EFL students:

a. differentiation between fact and opinion;
b. examination of assumptions, including their own; and
c. flexibility and open-mindedness whilst looking for explanations, causes, and solutions to problems.

A common misconception about critical thinking is that it means being a harsh critic. Actually, a critical thinker should be able to find reasons to praise an argument as well as reasons to criticize it.

One of the most basic skills taught in critical thinking courses is how to develop an argument. An argument has three parts: an issue, a conclusion, and a reason (or reasons). Students need to learn how to identify these in an essay. In addition, they need practice developing their own arguments.

Another skill is spotting logical fallacies. Students should become familiar with fallacies such as straw man, bandwagon, and slippery slope. They can learn to spot examples in political speeches and advertisements, as well as produce their own examples.

Critical thinking activities can be used to support students' language skills. Many features taught in critical thinking classes are quite useful in academic writing courses.

Use the activities in this chapter to develop students' critical thinking skills. The first five activities in this section work well together with brainstorming activities. Follow the guidelines from the beginning of the previous chapter to conduct a brainstorming session, then use one of the first five activities in this chapter to get students to choose the best solutions.

In later activities, students will learn how to develop strong arguments, think about how they form opinions, and take a critical look at advertising and news.

———

4.1 Ranking ideas

Aims – Writing, discussion, speaking, ranking
Time - 30 minutes
Preparation – Bring lots of post-it notes to class.

1. After conducting a brainstorming session, instruct each group to write all their solutions on post-it notes (one idea per note) and put them on a sheet of paper.

2. Have each group pass their paper to a different group.

3. The groups should rank the solutions and come up with a list of the top three, as well as the reasons they chose them.

4. Next, a member of each group should return the paper to the original group, and explain the choices they made.

5. Groups then discuss the top three chosen by the other group and decide if they want to change them or not.

6. In the final stage, each group should put their top three ideas on the board. Get students to vote for the best solution.

4.2 Scrutinizing solutions

Aims – Writing, discussion, speaking, ranking
Time - 1 hour
Preparation – Bring index cards, large sheets of blank paper, tape, and markers to class.

1. At the end of a brainstorming session, ask each student to put his or her best solution on an index card.

2. Pick these up, then give each student a card that belongs to another student.

3. Next, tell each student to consider the pros and cons of the solution written on the card.

4. Put students into groups of four or five. Ask them to read each other's cards and rank the solutions.

5. Give them a few minutes to decide on the best solution, then give each group a large sheet of poster paper and some markers. Tell them to make a poster which presents the solution and also describes the following items: 3 strengths of the solution, 3 weaknesses of the solution, 2 short-term consequences and 2 long-term consequences.

6. Give each group 15 minutes to produce the poster. Then have each group come to the front of the class to explain their poster to the class.

4.3 Solutions revisited

Aims – Writing, discussion, speaking, listening, ranking
Time – 1 hour
Preparation – Bring a lot of post-it notes to class.

1. After a brainstorming activity, ask students to write 5 solutions on 5 separate post-it notes. Tell them not to be concerned about how realistic the solution is, but to write down the first 5 solutions that come to mind.

2. Put a long horizontal line on the board, and write "most practical" on the left side and "least practical" on the right. Draw a vertical line in the middle. Tell students to put each post-it on the part of the line that represents the degree of practicality of their idea. They should not place any post-its on the vertical line in the middle.

3. Next, ask each student to take 2 post-it notes from the board. Tell them to choose one post-it from each side of the middle line.

4. Now ask them to take the solution that came from the practical side and find three reasons it might fail.

5. Then have them alter the solution that came from the impractical side to create a more useful idea.

6. Put student into pairs and ask them to discuss their work in steps 4 and 5.

7. Finally, call on a few students to tell the class about the two solutions they chose and what they did with them.

4.4 Creating criteria

Aims – Writing, discussion, speaking, ranking
Time - 45 minutes
Preparation – Bring a lot of post-it notes to class.

1. After doing a problem solving brainstorm, ask students to write 3 or 4 solutions on post-it notes, one solution per post-it.

2. Then draw a big 3 X 3 grid on the board. Tell the class they will use this grid to rank their solutions.

3. Put students into groups of six to think of 3 different criteria for judging solutions. These might include originality, usefulness, cost-effectiveness, simplicity, or any others your students can think of.

4. Ask groups to call out their criteria, as you write them on the board.

5. Next, get students to narrow down the list to two criteria they think are most important for judging their solutions.

6. Write one criterion on the left side of the grid with an arrow pointing up, and write the second above the grid with an arrow pointing to the left.

7. Now ask each group to put their post-its into one pile and pass them to another group.

8. Ask students to look over the other group's solutions carefully and place them where they think they belong in the matrix. If the solution is high in the criterion written on the left, it should be placed in the top row. And if a solution is high in the criterion written above the grid, it should go somewhere in the left column.

9. Now assign students to take one solution that ranks high in both criteria, and develop it into a paragraph for homework.

4.5 Pros, cons and fixes

Aims – Discussion, speaking, listening
Time - 45 minutes
Preparation - None

1. Once students have created several solutions to a problem in a brainstorming activity, have them do a pyramid discussion. This is done by first getting students to make a list of solutions individually. Then, put students in pairs to discuss possible solutions and choose their three best solutions. Next, put two pairs into a group of four to discuss their solutions and vote for the top three. After that, make two groups of four into a group of eight to further the discussion, culminating in a whole class discussion. Ask the entire class to choose the two best solutions to the problem.

2. Next tell them they're going to take a closer look at the first solution they chose.

3. Tell them they need to list all of the pros (strengths) of the first solution. Have students call them out as you write them on the board. Then have them call out all the cons (weaknesses). Now you write these on the board.

4. Tell students to point out any pros or cons that are identical in meaning and cross them out.

5. Now challenge your students to think of ways you can "fix" the cons to make them work. Write these "fixes" next to the cons.

6. Call on a student to come to the board and repeat steps 3-5 with the second solution.

7. Put students in pairs to discuss the two solutions.

8. Take a vote on which solution is the best. Ask several students why they voted the way they did.

Acknowledgement: I learned about the Pros-Cons-and-Fixes method from Morgan D. Jones' book *The Thinker's Toolkit*.

4.6 Facts and opinions

Aims – Listening, writing, discussion, writing, reading
Time - 20 minutes
Preparation - Create a list of 10 sentences, 5 facts and 5 opinions, based on a topic or reading covered in class recently. You should include a few opinions that are stated as facts, such as "Ice cream is delicious." or "U2 is the greatest rock band." Make copies of the discussion questions.

1. In class, dictate your list and have students write the sentences.

2. Ask students to write an "F" next to the facts and "O" next to the opinions.

3. Now put students in pairs to check their answers.

4. Ask students to write their sentences on the board. Call on several students to tell you which sentences are facts and which are opinions.

5. Put students in groups of three or four to discuss these questions:

> What is the major difference between facts and opinions?
> What words and phrases can be used to indicate whether a statement is a fact or an opinion?
> Why is it hard for some people to distinguish fact from opinion?
> Why do some people express their opinions as facts?
> What does it mean to say someone is "opinionated"?

6. Erase the board. As the discussion ends, call on students to go to the board and write a few notes about their discussion.

7. Finally, ask students to look at the statements on the board from step 6. Do they see more facts or opinions?

4.7 Probing beliefs

Aims – Writing, discussion
Time - 20 minutes
Preparation - Write these headings on the board: SCHOOL, FAMILY, PEER GROUP, RELIGION, GOVERNMENT. Make copies of the discussion questions.

1. When class begins, ask your students to think of several beliefs and values. Call on a few students to state some examples. Ask them if they can think of where their beliefs and values come from.

2. Tell them to take a sheet of paper, turn in sideways, and write the headings from the board on it. Ask students to write each of their beliefs under an appropriate heading.

3. Put them in pairs and ask them to share their charts.

4. Now put them in groups of 4 or 5 and have them discuss the following questions:

> Where do most of your beliefs come from?
> Tell your group about a belief that you changed. Why did you change it?
> What are your most strongly held beliefs?
> How do you feel when someone challenges your most strongly held beliefs?
> How do you deal with someone who has a very different belief system from you?
> What could you say to avoid a conflict with someone with different values?
> What's the difference between people who are very dogmatic and people who are more relativistic about their beliefs?

4.8 When you disagree

Aims – Reading, discussion, speaking, listening, writing
Time - 2 class periods (1st period - 5 minutes, 2nd period – 45 minutes)
Preparation - For homework, ask students to find an editorial that expresses an opinion they strongly disagree with. Tell them to bring a copy of the editorial to class next time. The website DailyOpEd (http://www.dailyoped.com/) has a wealth of editorials and opinion pieces.

1. In the next class period, write the following questions on the board. Ask students to read their editorial, and then think about the answers to these questions:

What was your first reaction when you started reading this article?
What do you think of the writer's style?
What percent of the article do you disagree with?
Are there any points in the article that you think are factually accurate?
What would you say to this writer if you had a chance to speak with him or her?
How do you feel about doing this kind of reading?

---

2. When they are finished reading, put them in groups of four or five to discuss their answers to the questions. Tell them you want one student in each group to take notes about the discussion and summarize the main points for the class.

3. After 10 minutes, call on each group to give their report. Ask each group some follow-up questions.

4. Finally, ask each group to think of one additional question to ask students in other groups about this assignment. Give each group a turn to address the others.

4.9 Teacher-led debate

Aims – Speaking, listening, language of agreement and disagreement, writing
Time - 20 minutes
Preparation - Prepare an argument that you think most of the class will disagree with. It should be somewhat controversial, but you need to prepare several arguments that support your position.

1. Give one student a marker, and invite the student to come to the whiteboard. Ask the student to write down two phrases in his own language to express agreement, and two phrases to express disagreement.

2. Then ask the student to choose a classmate to take his or her place. This second student needs to ask classmates to call out some English phrases that are used when you agree or disagree with someone, and write them on the board.

3. Once the class runs out of phrases, ask the second student to return to his or her seat. Write a few more phrases if there are not enough on the board.

4. Now, write the argument on the board. Read it out and give some supporting points.

5. Continue by asking a few students, "What do you think?" "Do you agree?"

6. Rebut some of their points, but give students plenty of freedom to disagree with you.

4.10 From dialogue to role play

Aims – Reading, writing, speaking, language of agreement and disagreement
Time - 30 minutes
Preparation - Before class, write the first part of a two-person debate on the board. It should state a strong opinion with a fact or example to back it up.

1. When class begins, call on a student to read out your statement as you write it on the board.

2. Tell students to imagine they disagree strongly. Call on a student to make a statement disagreeing with the first speaker. Write the words up on the board, correcting any errors.

3. Talk to another student and get that student to think up a response from the first speaker. Write in on the board. Continue until each speaker has 2 statements.

4. Divide your class into 2 groups. Give each student in the first group an envelope. Tell them to write their names on the front, one name per envelope. Collect them.

5. Give the second group a few sheets of paper. Tell them to write 3 statements about an issue on the left side of the page, similar to what you wrote on the board, but on a different issue.

6. While the second group is writing, collect the envelopes and ask the first group to come to the board. Tell them to write all the phrases they can think of for expressing an opinion ("In my opinion,... "I think..").

7. When the second group is finished writing, give each of them one of the envelopes from the first group. Ask each student to put the paper inside and deliver it to the student whose name is on it.

8. Now the first group should complete the dialogue, on the right side of the page, and then return it to the author. While the first group is writing, get the second group to go to the board and write all the phrases they can think of that express disagreement.

9. Put members of both groups together into pairs, and ask them to develop the dialogue into a role play. Give them 10 minutes to practice, then have each pair present its role play to the class.

4.11 Thinking fallacies

Aims – Reading, writing, speaking, listening
Time – 2 class periods (1st class - 10 minutes, 2nd class - 1 hour)
Preparation – None

1. At the beginning of class, write the following list on the board:

either-or thinking
straw man
hasty conclusion
faulty causation
attacking the person
bandwagon
slippery slope
false dilemma
appeal to reason

Next to the list, add this sentence: "You're either a winner or a loser."

2. Ask a student to read out the sentence. Tell the class that this is an example of a logical fallacy, known as either-or thinking. Give students a couple of minutes to think about why it is flawed. (Answer: there are many other options than being a winner or a loser, but the sentence makes it sound like they are the only two options.)

3. Next, read out the list to the class. Tell them that they are names of logical fallacies, where a writer is using faulty reasoning.

4. For homework, put students into small groups and give each group a different fallacy. Their task is to find the fallacy on the Internet and prepare a short presentation on it. Their presentation should include a clear, concise definition of the fallacy, as well as an example of it. They should go to one of these websites:

The Nizkor Project - Fallacies (www.nizkor.org/features/fallacies/)
Fallacy Files - Taxonomy of Logical Fallacies (www.fallacyfiles.org/taxonomy.html)
Stephen's Guide to the Logical Fallacies (onegoodmove.org/fallacy/welcome.htm)

5. In the next class, ask each group to present the fallacy they researched. Ask other students to take notes and ask questions after the presentations.

6. Finally put students into pairs. Ask each pair to create a dialogue based on one of the fallacies presented by other students in class.

7. Ask the pairs to read out their dialogues without naming the fallacy. Invite them to guess the fallacy depicted in the dialogue.

4.12 Emotion vs. reason

Aims – Speaking, listening, discussion
Time – 2 class periods (1st class - 5 minutes, 2nd class – 1.5 hours)
Preparation – Make copies of the two cards.

1. For homework, assign a debatable argument for students to produce arguments for and against. (One option is a topic related to your course that students are likely to disagree on, such as "The teacher should teach us in English only." or "We should use our coursebook more in class."). They should write down facts and information that support both sides of the issue. Tell them that in the next class they are going to have a debate.

2. In the next class period, put students in pairs, and ask them to take different sides of the issue. Give half the class the "A" cards and the other half the "B" cards. Tell them not to look at each other's cards.

> A. In this debate, you should use as few facts as possible. Concentrate on appealing to the emotions of the audience. Ridicule the opponent's position. Exaggerate everything so that your position sounds like the best one. Use your voice, body language, and facial expressions to make your words more dramatic.

> B. In this debate, you should use logic and reason in the debate. Only use the facts to support your point. Be honest and don't exaggerate anything.

3. Give students 10 minutes to prepare for the debate individually.

4. Now have each pair practice for the debate in their seats.

5. Next put the pairs together and have each pair present their debate to another pair.

6. Ask each group of four to send the best pair of debaters to debate in front of the class.

7. After the debates, have a whole-class discussion using the following questions:

What was the difference between the two participants of the debate?
How did their speaking style affect how you heard their message?
Who was the most effective speaker? Why?
What qualities do you prefer in a public speaker? Why?
Name a well-known speaker in your country. How would you describe him or her?

4.13 Praise and criticism

Aims – Reading, speaking, sharing criticism
Time - 30 minutes
Preparation – Make copies of a student's essay that expresses an opinion and is slightly controversial.

1. Put three chairs at the front of the classroom.

2. Ask students to call out some criteria by which a text can be judged. Write all their answers on the board. They should include such things as vocabulary, grammar, meaning, coherence, tone, and organization.

3. Give all students a copy of the text. Give them at least 10 minutes to read over the text and write some comments. They should include at least 3 positive comments and 3 negative comments, and they should be as specific as possible.

4. Call on three students to sit in the chairs. The student in the middle will read out the text, sentence by sentence. After the student in the middle reads a sentence, he or she will pause, and the student on the left will say something positive about the sentence (for example, uses good vocabulary, or flows well with the rest of the paragraph), while the student on the right will say something negative (for example, meaning not clear, or does not match the tone of the rest of the paragraph). Allow for the students on the left or right to skip a turn if they have trouble thinking of something to say.

5. After repeating the exercise with 4 sentences, ask the three students in the chairs to choose new students to sit there. Repeat several times until most or all of the students have had a chance to sit in front of the class.

6. Finally, after the entire text has been read, ask several students to go to the board and write any additional comments (positive and negative) about the text as a whole.

4.14 Weasel words

Aims – Reading, speaking, listening
Time - 30 minutes
Preparation – Make copies of articles and advertisements featuring weasel words

1. Ask your class for an example of a word or phrase that can be used deliberately to mislead. If they are not responsive, give them one or two examples from below.

2. Write *weasel words* on the board. Explain to the class that weasel words are words used by politicians and advertisers to deceive or mislead an audience. Tell them you are going to show them some examples, and let them guess what is wrong with them.

3. Put students into pairs. Write some of the following examples on the board, without the comments in parenthesis and have the pairs discuss them:

"Mistakes were made." (use of passive voice makes it unclear who made the mistakes)

"Studies show that...." (without actually seeing the studies, it's impossible to conclude anything)

"It helps control bad breath." (*helps* makes the rest of the statement unclear)

"Our product is the best." (*best* is a common weasel word, why is it the best?)

"Prizes up to 6 million dollars!" (*up to* emphasizes the best case)

"They reported some casualties." (*some* is too vague to be meaningful) "implementing functional actualization of the optimization threshold" (too much jargon, difficult to understand)

"Honestly speaking, I agree with him." (*honestly speaking* or *to be honest*, misleads the listener into thinking the speaker is being forthright)

4. Read out the examples and call on pairs to comment. Give them your answers when necessary.

5. Next put students into groups of three or four. Give each group a few of the articles you brought in and tell them to look for more examples of weasel words.

6. After 10 minutes, ask each group to present at least one example.

Follow-up: You can assign students to bring in their own examples of weasel words from articles.

4.15 Collaborative arguments

Aims – Reading, writing, organizing a paragraph
Time - 30 minutes
Preparation – None

1. Explain to your class the three parts of an argument: an issue, a conclusion and one or more reasons. Put an example on the board such as:

Issue: Government regulation of the Internet
Conclusion: The government should regulate content on the Internet
Reason: The government should protect children from being exposed to offensive materials on the Internet

2. Give each student a sheet of paper and ask them to write an issue (but not a conclusion or a reason) on their paper. Encourage them to choose controversial issues that everyone may not agree with. Give them a few minutes to write.

3. When they are finished, redistribute the papers so that everyone has another student's paper.

4. Ask students to write a conclusion based on the issue written on their paper.

5. Next redistribute the papers once again, and ask students to write 3 reasons that support the conclusion.

6. Invite several students to read out their arguments. Ask other students to comment on the strength of the arguments.

7. For homework, assign students to write a paragraph based on their arguments.

4.16 Where you stand

Aims – Writing, speaking, expressing opinions
Time - 20 minutes
Preparation – None

1. Write two statements on the far left and far right sides of the chalkboard. These statements should represent two opposing points of view on an issue. For example, on one side you might write "TV is garbage" and on the other side, "TV is educational."

2. Draw a horizontal line between the two statements.

3. Invite students to come to the board and write their names somewhere on the line, based on their opinions about the issue.

4. When everyone is finished, ask several students to share their opinions on the issue.

Follow-up: Ask a student to erase the two statements on the board and write two more opposing statements about a different issue. Repeat steps 3 and 4.

4.17 Devil's advocate

Aims – Speaking, listening, discussion
Time - 20 minutes
Preparation – None

1. Write a few controversial topics up on the board that you think your students will want to discuss. Encourage students to call out a few more. You write these up as well.

2. Put students in pairs. Tell them that one student will give his opinion on one of these topics, and the other will play devil's advocate. Explain that playing devil's advocate means deliberately challenging the other's words in order to provoke discussion. They should challenge the other student's opinions **even if they agree with the other student.**

3. Have them do this exercise for a few minutes, then switch roles.

4. Now ask a few students what they thought about playing devil's advocate.

4.18 Reading with roles

Aims – Reading, scanning, speaking
Time - 30 minutes
Preparation – Prepare copies of these cards:

LANGUAGE - Your task is to look for language that is misleading, vague, or confusing.

NUMBERS - Your task is to look for use of numbers and statistics that might be incorrect or distorted.

IMAGES - Your task is to look for pictures that might bias the reader.

ORDERING - Your task is to look for news articles where the order of the information that might bias the reader.

The number of cards should equal the number of students in your class. Also, bring four recent newspapers to class.

1. In class, tell students that they are going to look at newspapers in order to find things that might bias or mislead the reader.

2. Put students into groups of four, and give each student a newspaper. Hand out the cards, giving each group member a different card. Tell them to follow the task on their cards, then discuss with their group.

3. Have each group report their findings to the class.

4.19 The front page

Aims – Reading, discussion, speaking, summarizing, listening
Time - 20 minutes
Preparation – Bring the front pages of four newspapers, along with some tape. Tape up four front pages of newspapers in the four corners of your classroom. Make copies of the discussion questions. The website Newseum (www.newseum.org) features the front pages of newspapers from around the world.

1. When class begins, ask students to look at the different front pages and go to the one they like the most.

2. Ask students to stand in front of the page, and discuss with the other students why they chose it. Circulate and ask students questions.

3. Pass out copies of these discussion questions:

What made the front page you chose attractive to you?
What made the other ones less attractive?
What factors do newspaper editors consider when creating a front page?
Do any of these factors contradict the newspaper's role as a means of informing the public about important events?
How do these front pages compare with newspapers in your country?
If you could design an ideal front page, what would be on it? What would you leave out?

Put students in groups of five or six to discuss the questions. Ask one person to take notes. After 10 minutes, ask the note-taker in each group to visit another group and give a summary of the notes to the other group.

Follow-up: Ask students to design their own front pages and show them to the class.

4.20 Newspaper bar graph

Aims – Reading, writing, discussion, speaking, listening
Time – 1 hour
Preparation – Bring in enough English newspapers so that each group of four or five students can have one. Make copies of the discussion questions.

1. Put students in groups of four or five. Give each group a newspaper.

2. Ask students establish their own criteria for what constitutes important news. Tell students to look through the entire paper and examine how much of the paper meets their criteria.

3. Tell each group to create a bar graph that shows how much of the newspaper contains important news, and how much of it contains other things (advertising, entertainment news, etc.). Ask them to create their own categories for the bar graph.

4. Next, each group will present their bar graph to the class.

5. Pass out copies of these discussion questions:

> What was your reaction to the amount of important news in your newspaper?
> What type of news would you like to see more of? What would you like to see less of?
> Why do you think newspapers contain so many things other than important news?
> Can you recommend any news sources that provide more important news?
> What complaints do you have about the news media?
> How are newspapers different in your country?
> How has the Internet changed the way we read the news?

6. Ask students to read over the questions and write one more discussion question related to newspapers. Circulate as they write. Choose three students to put their questions on the board.

7. Now ask students to stand up in order of their age. Pair up students from both ends of the line. Continue until all students have been paired up. Ask each pair to go over the discussion questions.

8. After pairs have discussed all the questions, call on a few students to choose a question from the handout and answer it.

4.21 Two perspectives

Aims – Reading, scanning, discussion
Time - 30 minutes
Preparation – Make copies of two newspaper or magazine articles on the same subject for each student in the class. Ideally, both articles should cover the same event from a different perspective.

1. Put students in groups of three and ask them to look over both articles. Write these questions on the board and ask students to discuss them:

How are the two articles different?
Is there any information contained in one article, but missing in the other?
What might be the reason for this?
Do the articles indicate what their intended audiences are?
How might the intended audience shape the content of the article?

2. Have each group present their findings. Then ask the class which article they think presents a more reliable view and why.

4.22 Exploring advertising

Aims – Reading, speaking
Time - 2 class periods (1st class - 5 minutes, 2nd class - 30 minutes)
Preparation – Make copies of the questions for each student.

1. For homework, assign students to choose one advertisement (newspaper, magazine, TV, radio, billboard, etc.) and use the following questions to examine it:

What is the advertisement selling?
Do you think it is an effective advertisement? Why or why not?
What audience is the ad appealing to (men, women, young people, families)?
What elements of the ad do you think draw the public's attention?
What images are present in the ad? What is the importance of these images?
If it is a TV or radio ad, what sound elements (music, sound effects, voices) are present in the ad? What is the importance of these elements?
What words are used in the ad? Why were these words chosen?
Does the ad include a jingle (a catchy tune) or a catchphrase (a memorable phrase)? Have you heard it before?
Is there anything deceptive about the ad? What do you know about the product that, if mentioned in the ad, would make it less attractive to the consumer?
Is the product prominently featured in the ad, or is it almost invisible?
How do you think the advertisement would influence a consumer to buy the product?
What could you change to make the ad more effective in selling the product? What could you change to make the ad more honest?
Do you think the ad would be equally effective in another medium? Explain.
Would this ad be effective in your country? Why or why not?

Tell students the questions are provided to guide their thinking about the ad. If one question doesn't seem to relate to their ad, they can skip it.

2. In the next class period, call on students to present their ad to the class. Emphasize that you don't want them to read the questions off the handout and answer them, but to give a personal response to the ad, based on their thoughts and feelings.

4.23 Political cartoons

Aims – Reading, discussion, presentation
Time - 2 class periods (1st class - 5 minutes, 2nd class - 30 minutes)
Preparation - At the end of a class period, assign students to find a political cartoon and bring it to class next time.

1. In class, ask students to put their cartoons on a table to share with others. (You may wish to bring a few of your own, in case some students don't bring one.) Ask everyone to choose a cartoon other than the one they brought in.

2. Tell them to sit quietly and look over the cartoon. Write these questions on the board for students to discuss:

What is the cartoon trying to express? Summarize its point in a sentence or two.
What information does the cartoon overlook?
Do you think the cartoon is funny? Would it be funny in your culture?

3. Call on a few students to come to the front of the class, present their cartoon, and share their thoughts.

4.24 Shaping opinion

Aims – Reading, speaking, listening, discussion
Time - 30 minutes
Preparation - Before class, go to a website featuring movie reviews such as Metacritic (metacritic.com) or Rotten Tomatoes (rottentoma-toes.com) and choose a film which has both very positive and very negative reviews. For ideal results, choose an obscure film your students probably have not seen. Select a positive review and a negative review, and make copies for your next class. Also, make copies of the discussion questions.

1. In class, ask half the class to read one review, and the other half to read the other. Do not tell them anything about the review other than the title of the film.

2. Next, put students into pairs, making sure each pair contains two students who have read different reviews. Ask them to discuss the film.

3. After 5 minutes, halt the discussion, and ask a few pairs to relate how their discussion went. Explain to the class how you prepared the reviews they read.

4. Now put pairs into groups of 4, and give them a copy of the following questions to read and discuss:

> How often do you read reviews and criticism?
> What kind of reviews do you read? Book? Film? Restaurant?
> If you read a review before you see a film, do you think it will influence how you experience the film? Explain your answer.
> Do you think being a critic is a respectable job? Why or why not?
> Would you like to have a job as a critic? Why or why not?
> Have you ever written a review on a website? If you have, tell your group about it.
> In the U.S., some film critics, such as Roger Ebert, are celebrities. How are critics perceived in your country?

Follow-up: Ask students to read reviews for homework, and write down some useful language from the reviews.

Variation: You can do this activity with book reviews or CD reviews.

———

For The Teacher

Vincent Ryan Ruggiero is an expert on critical thinking, having written several well-known books on the subject. In this interview, he gives us an overview of his career teaching and writing about critical thinking. In addition, he provides some useful suggestions for teachers who want to develop their students' critical thinking skills.

Vincent Ryan Ruggiero on Critical Thinking

Vincent Ryan Ruggiero, Professor Emeritus of Humanities at SUNY-Delhi, is a widely known author and lecturer. His book titles include college, trade, and professional publications. His areas of expertise are critical thinking, creative thinking, ethics, communication, and curriculum reform and staff development. Ruggiero made his reputation within the academic world by pioneering the movement to make thinking skills instruction a necessary emphasis at every level of education.

What got you interested in critical thinking?

A happy accident. In 1957, having completed a rather typical liberal arts program, with an emphasis on English and philosophy, I took a position as an industrial engineer ("efficiency expert") with a large company. My job consisted of doing time and motion studies to determine the simplest and most efficient way to do various tasks. If you've ever watched people work, even without a stop watch in your hand, you've probably noticed that some people accomplish more than others in the same time period. This applies to everyday tasks, such as preparing a meal, ironing shirts, or washing the car, as well as to the tasks associated with the workplace.

Why do some people perform so much better than others? The most important factor is not inborn talent or years of experience. It's the way they perform the tasks—the number, complexity, and difficulty of the motions they employ. When we eliminate useless motions and streamline the others, we save energy, time, and in many cases, money. Time and motion studies help companies make those savings.

My job as an industrial engineer also involved studying the equipment and layout of a workplace. When I studied an operation, I asked such questions as these: Are the right tools being used? Is the workplace arranged to promote efficient performance? Would new equipment help? Is such equipment available for purchase? If not, can a new piece of equipment be designed? (In one case, I designed a new sorting table that permitted workers to handle returned merchandise more easily and efficiently.)

I also monitored the performance of entire departments. Whenever a department was spending more than the hours and dollars allocated for its function—I analyzed the work records to determine the cause. Often I could trace the problem to inefficient use of employee time, such as having highly paid technical employees working on tasks that should have been done by lower-paid employees.

The essence of my work as an industrial engineer was *creative and critical* thinking. Those words were not yet widely used, of course. Some scholars had written about critical thinking and "productive" thinking, but their work had little impact on industry or education at that time.

Did you see the connection of what you were doing to the field of education?

Not at the time. I should mention that during the four years I was an engineer, I was also pursuing graduate studies in English at night. When I received my degree, I took a teaching position in a college humanities department. My main teaching assignments were in composition and literature. Before long, I realized that my conception of education was different from the conceptions of my colleagues. I believed that my role was not merely to present subject matter to students but to teach them how to think about that subject matter. (Teaching students *how* to think is, of course, very different from telling them *what* to think.)

In the case of teaching composition, I regarded my job as twofold: not just guiding students to express their thoughts well, with proper regard for the rules of organization, syntax, and grammar; but also helping them discover thoughts that are worthy of expression. In other words, I regarded rhetoric not merely as *form* but also, and more importantly, as *substance*.

I soon decided that *every* course and curriculum should have as its principal aim the teaching of thinking. For examples, history instruction should guide students in asking the questions historians ask, searching for answers as historians search, and making judgments as historians make them. Imparting factual knowledge should be subordinate to thinking instruction.

When did you begin writing books on critical thinking?

Early in my teaching experience, I began developing my own materials for teaching reasoning and persuasion, mainly because few good published materials were available. Then I attended a national conference on composition instruction hoping to find materials that were more sophisticated and effective than the ones I had designed. In fact, I found that my materials were superior, so I wrote my first textbook, *The Elements of Rhetoric* (1971), which included organization and style but gave greater emphasis to reasoning and persuasion.

Many other books followed, notably *Thinking Critically About Ethical Issues*, originally titled *The Moral Imperative* (1973); *Beyond Feelings: A Guide to Critical Thinking* (1975); *The Art of Thinking* (1984); and *Becoming a Critical Thinker* (1989). I mention these four books because each has been continuously in print, in various editions, since it was introduced. (Incidentally, *The Art of Thinking* is now available in a Chinese edition.)

I have written books on other subjects, as well. For example, a handbook for teachers entitled *Teaching Thinking Across the Curriculum* (1985); a work of social criticism, *Warning: Nonsense Is Destroying*

America (1994); and a guide to more meaningful living, *The Practice of Loving Kindness* (2003). But my textbooks on critical thinking are better known.

What is your definition of critical thinking?

Since critical thinking is one of three important kinds of thinking, let me begin with my definition of *thinking* in general: "Thinking is any mental activity that helps formulate or solve a problem, resolve an issue, or fulfill a desire to understand. It is a searching for answers, a reaching for meaning."

Philosophers, notably logicians, have been especially interested in *critical* thinking, the essence of which is the evaluation of ideas. Psychologists have been especially interested in *creative* thinking, the processes by which ideas are produced.

Unfortunately, relatively few individuals have been interested in the interactions between critical and creative thinking, and even fewer in the relationship of the third kind of thinking, *reflective* thinking, to the other two. Over the years I have become increasingly interested in these relationships, which may be roughly described as follows: Reflective thinking ponders experience and identifies interesting problems and issues; Creative thinking applies imagination and produces possible solutions and resolutions; and Critical thinking compares the solutions and resolutions and determines which are most reasonable and/or practical.

What do you think is the best way to teach critical thinking?

It depends on the type of course, the specific goals of the instructor, and the time available to devote to critical thinking instruction. As Edward Glaser wrote in *An Experiment in the Development of Critical Thinking*: "Almost any subject or project can be so taught as to put pupils on guard against generalization, contradictory assertions, and the uncritical acceptance of authority . . . In general the research indicates that if the objective is to develop in pupils an attitude of 'reasonableness' and regard for the weight of evidence and to develop ability to think critically about controversial problems, then the component attitudes and abilities involved in thinking critically about such problems must be set up as definite goals of instruction." That book was written more than half a century ago but remains a source of insights for educators.

On the other hand, Glaser warned against the unfortunately common notion that certain courses—science, for example—teach critical thinking *automatically*. There are no such courses. Ironically, a course could be titled critical thinking and yet not be teaching critical thinking. How? By having the instructor spend every class period lecturing about critical thinking and assigning homework that requires nothing more than reading other people's ideas about critical thinking.

I've often used a sports analogy to explain this point. Imagine a basketball team that never practiced passing, shooting, running plays, and never had a scrimmage, but simply sat in the bleachers and listened to their coaches lecture about basketball terminology or regale them with stories of great games of the past. Such a team might know a lot *about* basketball but they wouldn't learn how to play the game.

In thinking as in basketball, "propositional" knowledge (facts and principles) has its place, but excellence is measured by performance skill. Thus, the first step in teaching critical thinking is to provide students with a "heuristic," or strategy for thinking. The next step is to have them apply the strategy to a variety of problems and issues. Lots of them.

Can you give some suggestions for teachers who want to teach critical thinking?

The most important suggestion is this: When choosing challenges for students, never use issues that you have strong feelings about. This advice goes against teachers' natural inclinations, I realize. For example, if you have strong feelings for or against capital punishment, you will want to choose it as an issue. If you do so, however, you will be tempted to slip from the role of guide to the role of advocate. Before you know it, you will no longer be helping students investigate both sides of the issue, evaluate the various pro and con arguments, and form reasonable judgments. Instead, you will be trying to persuade them that your personal view is the correct one. Instead of teaching critical thinking, you'll be brainwashing students. I've seen many teachers make this mistake.

There's another reason this suggestion is important. One of the key lessons in learning how to think well is overcoming one's preconceptions, unwarranted assumptions, and biases. This is not an easy task, so students will need your good example to help them achieve it. You are best able to give that example when you are not emotionally involved with the issues under discussion.

Some readers might be thinking, "If I rule out subjects I feel strongly about, such as capital punishment, abortion, creationism, and the current administration in Washington, what subjects are left?" The answer is *all kinds of issues* from campus issues to local, national, and international issues. Listen to any newscast or check any newspaper op-ed page, and you'll find plenty of issues of interest to students, including the parking situation on campus and the quality and variety of the food in the cafeteria.

Another suggestion to instructors: Keep your intrusions into class discussions minimal. Instead of explaining everything that needs explaining, ask students to explain. If a response is insufficient, or an opinion shallow or biased, ask the class to comment on it, so that they can gain the insight. They will profit more from that approach than they will when all the insights come from you.

A third suggestion: In the vast majority of cases, it is best if students don't know your personal view of issues. If they try to guess, disguise your view by stating a strong argument on one side of the issue and an equally strong argument on the other side and then ask them to judge which of those arguments is better, or whether they can think of *another* argument that is even better than those two. If you keep the emphasis on their thinking processes rather than yours, you will not only give them valuable practice in solving problems and making decisions; you will also help them to become more independent thinkers. And that, after all, is a central aim of critical thinking instruction.

———

Further reading

Books

Moore, B. N. and Parker, R. (2007). *Critical thinking*. Boston: McGraw Hill.

Ruggiero, V. R. (2004). *Beyond feelings*. New York: McGraw Hill.

Websites

The Critical Thinking Community
http://www.criticalthinking.org/

Critical Thinking on the Web
http://www.austhink.org/critical/

5
Organizing Ideas on Paper

This chapter introduces a myriad of ways for students to record and develop their ideas in writing. These are highly suitable for visual learners or classes which emphasize writing.

The first section, Working With Topics and Texts, contains several traditional graphic organizers such as KWHL and timelines. These can aid students in exploring a text or organizing ideas.

The second section, Generating Ideas, concentrates on creative skills. These give students opportunities to produce new ideas, and work together on short projects.

The third section, Getting Feedback, allows the teacher to collect students' thoughts and opinions and find out what students really think about their classes.

The first six activities in this chapter are graphic organizers. While graphic organizers have traditionally been used in first language classrooms, Stoller (2007) points out a number of aims that make them useful in the L2 classroom as well. These include connecting new information with previously learned information, organizing and summarizing information from a multitude of sources, reviewing, involving students in group work, and diagnosing what students know and don't know. Visual learners, who prefer to work with charts and graphs, will respond well to using graphic organizers. The following activities are a sample of a large number of graphic organizers that can aid the language learning process. An alternative to photocopying diagrams is to draw the graphic organizer on the board, and then let students copy it on their own paper.

———

WORKING WITH TOPICS AND TEXTS

5.1 Venn diagram

Aims – Discussion, speaking, listening, writing
Time - 30 minutes
Preparation – None

1. Choose two topics you have discussed with students in previous lessons. Ideally, these two topics should not be too similar.

2. Draw two large overlapping circles on the board, and get students to do the same. Explain to the class that this is a Venn diagram. Ask them to write one of the two topics above each circle.

3. Tell them to think of things that are different about the topics and write these in the circles under the appropriate heading. They should not write in the space where the two circles overlap.

4. Next, ask them to think of ways the two topics are similar and write these in the space in the middle where the two circles overlap or just below it.

5. Put students into pairs and have them compare their Venn diagrams.

6. Finally, call on three students to come to the board and reproduce their Venn diagrams.

5.2 KWHL technique

Aims – Speaking, listening, forming questions, writing, reading, reviewing an article

Time - 1 hour

Preparation – Prepare copies of an article about a topic you think will appeal to your students.

1. Announce the topic of your article. Go around the class and ask each student to say a word he or she thinks might be in the article.

2. Make a chart with four columns on the board. At the top of each column write the letters K, W, H, and L (one per column). Ask students to copy the chart on their own paper. Next, give them a few minutes to write down what they already know about the topic in the first column. (This is the K column, which stands for What We Already Know.)

3. Call on a student to ask another student to read out one thing he or she wrote down. Repeat until about half the students have read out something.

4. Get students to call out some question words (who, what, when, where, why). Write them up on the board, and add other words that can start a question (did, is, was, should, will).

5. Ask students to think of 5 questions that they would like to have answered on this topic. Tell them to write the questions in the second column. (This is the W column, which stands for What We Would Like to Know.)

6. Tell the class to think of ways they could get answers to their questions. In the next column, students need to write down several ideas on how they could gather more information on this subject. (This is the H column, which stands for How We Can Learn More.) Ask them to be as specific as possible. For example, if your topic is sharks, it's better to write "do a web search with the keywords SHARK FACTS" than to just write "do a web search".

7. Now give them the reading. Ask them to look for answers to their questions.

8. After they have had time to read, ask students to raise their hands if the article answered one or more of their questions. Assign several students to write a question and the answer on the board.

9. Ask students to write down several things they learned in the third column. They should write any new information, even if it didn't directly answer one of their questions. (This is the L column, which stands for What We Learned.)

10. Finally, put students in groups of 4 to share their KWHL charts.

5.3 Storyboard

Aims – Speaking, reading, writing, reviewing a story
Time - 30 minutes
Preparation – None

1. Go over a story or a movie you discussed in class recently. Call on students to tell you the most important plot points.

2. Draw nine squares on the board (3 X 3) and tell the class to do the same on their own paper. Ask them to work in pairs to summarize the plot. They need to draw pictures in the boxes, and write a one-sentence summary at the bottom of each box.

3. When they're finished, have them put their storyboards on the walls. Ask everyone to stand up and look at the different storyboards.

4. When everyone's returned to their seats, ask a few students to point out similarities and differences between some of the storyboards.

5.4 Timeline

Aims – Reading, writing, reviewing a text, listening, speaking, sharing personal information
Time – 1 hour
Preparation – Make copies of an article that discusses a historical period, or the events in the life of a famous person.

1. Introduce students to timelines by drawing a long horizontal line on the board, and adding important dates and events from your own life. Briefly explain some of them to the class.

2. Give students copies of the article. Ask them to underline the major events and dates mentioned in the article.

3. Ask students to produce their own timelines for the article and mark the most important dates.

4. Get students to compare their timelines in pairs.

5. Next, ask one student to come to the board and work together with the class to make a timeline for the article on the board.

6. Now ask students to think of the most important events in their own lives. Call on a few students to share with the class.

7. Assign students to make timelines of their lives. Ask them to add one false event.

8. When they're finished, they should put their timelines up on the walls. Everyone should circulate and look over the timelines. Can they spot the false event?

9. Go over each timeline with the class. Call on students to identify the false events.

5.5 Five W's and H

Aims – Writing, speaking, constructing a paragraph
Time – 30 minutes
Preparation – Prepare 6 questions related to a topic, using the question words who, what, when, where, why and how.

1. Ask your class if they know the 6 question words (Who, What, When, Where, Why, How). Have a student write them on the board.

2. Tell students that these questions are often used in journalism to develop a story. You will introduce the class to how they can expand their own writing with these questions.

3. Give students a topic. Ask them to create a chart with 6 columns. They should put one of the question words at the top of each column. For each question word, read out a question, then ask them to write two more. Here are some examples:

Topic: Online music

Who – Who is the most downloaded artist in music today?
What – What steps do we take to download music from the Internet?
When – When do most students in this class listen to music online?
Where – Where can you go online to download music?
Why – Why do people prefer to get music online instead of buying a CD?
How – How can we find the latest hits online?

4. Ask students to compare their questions with a partner. Also, ask them to collaborate with their partners to produce one more question in each category.

5. Put the words up as headings on the board. Call on students to contribute their questions, until all columns have several questions. Make corrections if necessary.

6. For homework, ask students to find the answers to some of these questions, and put the answers together into a paragraph.

Variations:

- ask students to write personal questions they would like to ask each other, then get students to stand up and mingle, using the questions they wrote.

- give students a dramatic first sentence to a short story. Assign them to write questions about the first sentence, and produce their own answers. They can then use the answers to write their own stories.

5.6 Step-by-step chart

Aims - Describing a process, using detail, writing
Time - 30 minutes
Materials - None

1. Write up on the board a few examples of things that can be explained as a step-by-step process, such as planning a party, making a cake, changing a baby's diapers, or preparing for a hurricane. Call on students to think of even more examples and add these to your list.

2. Put students into groups of 5 or 6. Each group needs to choose a process and make some notes on all the steps in the process. They also need to write down specific details for each step. Ask each group to transform their notes into a chart containing a box for each step. Also, they should include a list of materials and costs related to the process.

3. When students are finished, tell them to tape their charts to the board. Encourage everyone to read and add comments and suggestions for improvement.

Follow-up: Ask students to create an essay about the process using the notes on their charts.

More Ideas for Using Graphic Organizers

Here are some additional ways you can use graphic organizers with your class:

1. After reading or listening, hand out a completed graphic organizer that contains a few errors. Put students in pairs to find the errors and correct them.

2. Prepare two versions of a graphic organizer, both partially completed, but each with answers that are missing on the other organizer. Seat students back to back, and instruct them to ask each other questions to complete both graphic organizers.

3. Assign one student to prepare a lecture about a topic that interests him or her. After the lecture, have the other students fill out an appropriate graphic organizer.

4. Give students a completed graphic organizer and have them develop it into a paragraph.

5. Make a large graphic organizer on the board or on a huge sheet of blank paper. Invite students to come up and fill it in.

6. Put students in a circle. Give each student a graphic organizer. Ask students to fill in the first part, then pass it to the next student to add more information. Continue until all the organizers are complete.

GENERATING IDEAS

5.7 Idea constellation

Aims – Brainstorming, writing, developing ideas, introducing a topic
Time – 45 minutes
Preparation – None

1. In the center of the board, write the name of a topic you want to cover and circle it. Call on a student to think of a word that relates to the topic. Ask the student to write the word near the topic, draw a box around it, then draw an arrow from the topic to the new word. Repeat this procedure with other students until there are eight words surrounding the topic.

2. Choose a student to write the eight words from step 1 on the sides of the board (two at the top, two at the bottom, two on the left, and two on the right).

3. Put students into eight groups. Assign each group one of the words. Their task is to think of three phrases (3 to 5 words) they associate with their word. They should write these phrases near their word on the board, draw a triangle around each phrase, and draw arrows from the word to the phrases.

4. Next erase the topic and words in the center of the board, leaving the words and phrases on the sides.

5. Write the following words and phrases on the board: to begin with, in addition to, however, nevertheless, while, as well as, not only, ultimately.

6. Put students into pairs and ask them to use the words on the board to construct a three sentence paragraph.

7. After a few minutes, call on three groups to write their paragraphs on the board.

8. Work together with the class to find ways to improve these paragraphs.

5.8 Attribute listing

Aims – Language of description, writing, speaking
Time – 1 hour
Preparation – Bring poster paper and your cell phone to class.

1. At the beginning of class, hold up your cell phone. Tell students you want them to each think of seven different properties of a cell phone. Give them a couple of examples, such as size and color. (They might come up with price, ringtone, shape, material, function, weight, and texture.)

2. Put students into groups of three. Tell each group to assemble a list of five properties they think are the most important and add SPECIAL FUNCTION as the sixth one. Ask them to write the properties on a horizontal line at the top of a sheet of paper, leaving plenty of room at the bottom.

3. Next, ask groups to make a column under each heading and draw horizontal lines to make a grid. They need to write as many different ideas as they can think of. For example, in the COLOR column, they would write pink, blue, orange, yellow, and gray. In the SPECIAL FUNCTION column, they need to think of some unique special function that no other cell phone has.

4. After the groups have filled out most of the columns, assign them to create a revolutionary cell phone with some amazing properties that will make everyone want to buy it. First, students should look at all columns and choose a winning combination of properties. They don't need to use all the properties. Next, they need to create a poster to advertise the cell phone, and prepare to tell the class about what makes it so special.

5. Before each group makes their presentation, tell the other students to listen carefully and prepare questions to ask at the end of the pre-

sentation. Call on two or three students after each presentation to ask questions.

Variations: Instead of creating a new cell phone, they can create a new book, sandwich, running shoe, computer, watch, or car.

5.9 Creating the ultimate

Aims - Brainstorming, discussion, writing
Time - 45 minutes
Materials - None

1. Ask students for ideas for a short project which can be sketched on paper. Some possibilities include building a new school, creating a disco, designing a weapon, or even producing a monster.

2. Write their suggestions on the board and add a few of your own.

3. Now students will vote on a project to work on. Invite them to the board, and ask them to put a check mark next to any idea that interests them. Work together with the class to settle on one project from the ones with the most checks.

4. Put students in groups of 4 or 5. Ask each group to write "CREATE THE ULTIMATE _____" at the top of the page, completing the phrase with the aim of the project. They need to work together to draw a sketch of the completed project. It should include labels for different parts of the sketch. Also, one member of each group will give a report on their project to the class.

5. Tell the groups to discuss some ideas for a few minutes before writing anything down.

6. Circulate and ask the groups about their progress. Make sure that they label their drawings.

7. When all groups are finished, have a member of each group present to the class. After each presentation, ask a few students from other groups to give their impression of the project.

Variations

- allow each group to choose a completely different project

- put students into 3 groups. Each group draws the left side (1/3) of the project. Groups pass their papers to the next group, who completes the middle section. They exchange once more to finish.

GETTING FEEDBACK

5.10 Consensogram

Aims – Giving feedback on a course, speaking, fluency practice
Time - 10 minutes
Preparation – Bring a large blank poster and small dot stickers to class. Also, think of a subject you would like students to give you feedback on. Make it into a question, such as "How do you feel about doing role plays in class?" or "What do you think of our coursebook?" Write the question at the top of a blank poster. At the bottom write three or four statements such as "I love it!", "It's okay", "I'm not too crazy about it." and "I can't stand it".

1. Put the poster up on the board.

2. Get students to come up to the poster and put a dot sticker above the appropriate statement. The dots should be lined up into a column, starting at the bottom of the poster.

3. Once students return to their seats, encourage them to explain their thoughts on the topic. Ask follow-up questions, and allow for disagreement.

Follow-up: If you wish, you can repeat the activity once or more with the same poster to take note of any changes of opinion. Each time you repeat the activity, you should write the date, and use different pens for emphasis. Alternatively, you can use a different poster and a different topic each time.

5.11 Plus/Delta

Aims – Giving feedback on a course, writing
Time - 15 minutes
Preparation – Make copies of the handout.

1. Ask the class to think about how the class has been going so far. Tell them to concentrate on what helps them learn.

2. Pass out the handouts. Ask students to write down what they think is going right in the course in the left (plus) column.

3. Then ask them to write down what changes they would like to see in the right (delta) column.

4. Collect their papers and tell the class you will read them before the next class period.

Follow-up: In the next class period, give students some feedback about their comments.

5.12 Parking lot

Aims – Giving feedback on a course, writing, discussion, speaking, listening
Time - 30 minutes
Preparation – Bring post-it notes, tape, and a large blank poster (optional)

1. Tell students you want some comments about how they like the class so far.

2. Draw the parking lot diagram on the board or on a large poster. Tell them the box on the upper left is for comments on what is going well. The box on the upper right is for things that need improvement. The box on the lower left is for questions. The box on the lower right is for suggestions on how to improve the class.

3. Encourage them to stand up and write comments in each of the boxes. In a large class, you can distribute post-its, have students write on them, and then put the post-its in the appropriate boxes.

4. When students have stopped writing, read out some of the messages and invite students to tell you more.

5.13 Categorizing feedback

Aims - Giving feedback on a course, writing, discussion
Time - 20 minutes
Preparation - Bring a lot of post-its to class

1. Tell the class you want them to reflect on how the class has been going. Give them a few minutes of think time.

2. Give each student 4 post-its, and ask students to write a different comment on each post-it.

3. When they're finished, tell students to put their post-its on the board.

4. Next, assign students to discuss some categories for the comments. Don't suggest any categories, but allow them to think of categories on their own.

5. Once they have agreed on their categories, tell them to put the post-its into their chosen categories, and write the categories next to them.

6. Use these questions to guide a discussion:

Which comments came up the most?
Which category had the most comments? Why?
Which category had the fewest comments? Why?
What are some other categories you might have used?
Are there any comments you would like to elaborate on?
Is there anything you didn't write down that you'd like to express now?

5.14 Linking feedback

Aims - Giving feedback on a course, writing, reading
Time - 30 minutes
Preparation - None

1. Invite students to think about the class so far.

2. Give each student in the front row a sheet of paper. Assign these students to write a sentence or two about the course at the top of the page. Emphasize they need to write small, as other students will be writing on the paper as well.

3. Next, ask students to pass their papers to the students behind them. These students have two options. They can either add to the previous student's notes, or they can write about a different aspect of the course.

4. Repeat step 3 until the last row has added their comments. Provide students with additional sheets of paper if they run out of room to write.

5. Students in the last row put their papers up on the board. They should leave lots of space on the board between papers.

6. Bring all students to the board. Now, students should leave comments on the papers written by students in other rows.

7. After everyone has returned to their seats, take a minute to look over all the notes. Read out some of the comments, and ask a few students to share their thoughts.

5.15 Feedback on activities

Aims - Giving feedback on a course, speaking, discussion
Time - 20 minutes
Preparation - None

1. On the left side of the board, write out short descriptions of activities that you have done in class recently. Go over the list with the students, and make sure they remember them.

2. Ask students to come to the board and put a check next to any activities that they enjoyed. Also, tell them to put Xs next to any activities they did not enjoy.

3. When they are finished, ask students about activities that seem particularly popular or unpopular. Ask follow-up questions to learn more about what the students prefer.

5.16 Opus box

Aims - Giving feedback on a course, dictation, writing
Time - 15 minutes
Preparation - Prepare about ten sentences that describe aspects of your class you would like feedback on. For example, "This class is fun.", "The teacher corrects our mistakes.""The course materials are interesting." Also, bring four envelopes or boxes, each with one of the following labels: "agree", "somewhat agree", "disagree", and "no comment". Bring 10 index cards for each student.

1. Pass out the index cards, and tell the class you want to do a dictation. Tell them to write each sentence you dictate on a different card.

2. After the dictation, call on several students to write the sentences on the board. Correct any errors.

3. Now tell students to put the cards in the appropriate box or envelope. (You might do this at the end of class, and allow students to leave once they've turned in their cards.)

4. After class look over the cards and reflect on the student's feedback. Plan on discussing the feedback with the class at a later date.

Variation: you can give students a few extra cards to write their own statements.

Acknowledgement: I first encountered the Opus Box idea in Michael Michalko's *Thinkertoys*.

———

Further reading

Books

Bellanca, J. 2007. *A guide to graphic organizers*. Thousand Oaks, CA: Corwin Press.

Burke, J. 2002. *Tools for thought*. Portsmouth, NH : Heinemann.

Websites

University of Minnesota – Content-Based Language Teaching with Technology – Graphic Organizers
http://www.carla.umn.edu/cobaltt/modules/strategies/gorganizers/index.html

Schools of California Online Resources for Education - Graphic Organizers
http://www.sdcoe.k12.ca.us/SCORE/actbank/torganiz.htm

BIBLIOGRAPHY

Aleinikov, A. G. 2002. *Megacreativity*. Cincinnati, OH: Walking Stick Press.

Allen, R. 2005. *Boost your creativity*. London: Collins and Brown.

Anderson, L. W. and David R. Krathwohl, D. R., et al (Eds..) 2001. *A taxonomy for learning, teaching, and assessing*. Boston, MA.: Allyn & Bacon.

Baddeley, A. 2004. *Your memory*. New York: Firefly.

Bowkett, S. 2006. *100 ideas for teaching thinking skills*. London: Continuum.

Browne, M. N. and Keeley, S. M. 2007. *Asking the right questions*. Upper Saddle River, N.J.: Pearson Prentice Hall.

Chamot, A. U., Barnhardt, S. El-Dinary, P. B., and Robbins, J. 1999. *The learning strategies handbook*. New York: Pearson.

Clegg, B. 1999. *Instant brainpower*. London: Kogan Page, Ltd.

Clegg, B. and Birch, P. 1999. *Instant creativity*. London: Kogan Page, Ltd.

Cotton, K. 1991. Close-Up #11: Teaching Thinking Skills. Retrieved November 24, 2008, from Northwest Regional Educational Laboratory's School Improvement Research Series Web site: http://www.nwrel.org/scpd/sirs/6/cu11.html

Cottrell, S. 2005. *Critical thinking skills*. New York: Palgrave Macmillan.

Cowley, S. 2004. *Getting the buggers to think*. London: Continuum.

Crawford, A., Saul, E. W., Mathews, S. R., and Makinster, J. 2005. *Teaching and learning strategies for the thinking classroom*. New York: The International Debate Education Association.

Cullen, B. 1998. Brainstorming before speaking tasks. *The Internet TESL Journal*, Vol. IV, No. 7.

Day, R. R. 2003. Teaching critical thinking and discussion. *The Language Teacher*, 27 (7).

Diestler, S. 2005. *Becoming a critical thinker*. Upper Saddle River, N.J.: Pearson/Prentice Hall.

Dornyei, Z. and Murphey, T. 2003. *Group dynamics in the language classroom*. Cambridge: Cambridge University Press.

Epstein, R. 1999. Generativity theory. Runco, M. A. and Pritzker, S. (Eds.), *Encyclopedia of creativity*. New York: Academic Press, pp. 759-766.

Foord, D. 2009. *The developing teacher*. Surrey: Delta Publishing.

Fried- Booth, D. 2002. *Project work*. Oxford: Oxford University Press.

Furnham, A. 2000. The brainstorming myth. *Business Strategy Review*, 11 (4). Pp. 21-28.

Godwin, M. 2000. *Who are you?* New York: Penguin Books.

Hale-Evans, R. 2006. *Mind performance hacks*. Sebastopol, California: O'Reilly Media, Inc.

Harrison, A. F. and Bramson, R. M. 1982. *The art of thinking*. New York: Berkley.

Hennessey, B. A. and Amabile, T.. M. 1987. *Creativity and learning*. Washington, D.C.: National Education Association.

Herrmann, D., Raybeck, D., and Gruneberg, M. 2002. *Improving memory and study skills*. Seattle: Hogrefe and Huber Publishers.

Higbee, K. L. 1996. *Your memory*. New York: Marlowe.

Higgins, J. M. 1994. *101 creative problem solving techniques*. Winterpark, Florida: New Management Publishing.

Houston, H. 2007. *The creative classroom*. Toronto: Lynx Publishing.

Hulstijn, J. 1997. Mnemonic methods in foreign language vocabulary learning: Theoretical considerations and pedagogical implications. In Coady, J. and Huckin, T. (eds.) *Second language vocabulary acquisition* (Pp. 203-224). Cambridge: Cambridge University Press.

Jay, R. 2000. *The ultimate book of business creativity*. Oxford: Capstone Publishing.

Jiang, X. and Grabe, W. 2007. Graphic organizers in reading instruction: research findings and issues. *Reading in a Foreign Language*, 19 (1), pp 34-55.

Jones, M. D. 1998. *The thinker's toolkit*. London: Times Business.

Kabilan, M. K. 2000. Creative and critical thinking in language classrooms. *The Internet TESL Journal*, Vol. 6.

Khan, A. 1999. *Self help stuff that works*. Bellevue, WA: YouMe Works.

Kida, T. E. 2006. *Don't believe everything you think*. Amherst, NY: Prometheus.

Kirby, G. and Goodpaster, J. 2002. *Thinking*. New Jersey: Prentice Hall.

Lieberman, D. A. 2004. *Learning and memory*. Belmont, CA: Wadsworth Thomson Learning.

Lindstromberg, S. 1990. *The recipe book*. Canterbury: Pilgrims.

Majaro, S. 1988. *The creative gap*. London: Longman.

Mason, D. J. and Smith, S. X. 2005. *The memory doctor*. Oakland: New Harbinger Publications.

Meddings, L. and Thornbury, S. 2009. *Teaching unplugged*. Surrey: Delta Publishing.

Michalko, M. 2001. *Cracking creativity*. Berkeley, CA: Ten Speed Press.

Michalko, M. 2006. *Thinkertoys*. Berkeley, CA: Ten Speed Press.

Middleton, J. 2006. *Upgrade your brain*. Oxford: The Infinite Ideas Company Limited.

Moore, B. N. and Parker, R. 2007. *Critical thinking*. Boston: McGraw Hill.

O'Brien, D. 2001. *Learn to remember*. San Francisco: Chronicle Books.

Oxford, R. 1990. *Language learning strategies*. New York: Newbury House.

Richards, J. C. and Lockhart, C. 1994. *Reflective teaching in second language classrooms*. Cambridge: Cambridge University Press.

Rinvolucri, M. 2003. *Humanising your coursebook*. Surrey: Delta Publishing.

Ruggiero, V. R. 1988. *Teaching thinking across the curriculum*. New York: Harper and Row.

Ruggiero, V. R. 2008. *Beyond feelings*. New York: McGraw Hill.

Ruggiero, V. R. 2007. *The art of thinking*. New York: Pearson Longman.

Schachter, D. L. 2002. *The seven sins of memory*. New York: Houghton Mifflin.

Scrivener, J. 2005. *Learning teaching*. Macmillan.

Sharifian, F. 2002. Memory enhancement in language pedagogy: implications from cognitive research. *TESL-EJ*, 6 (2).

Small, G. 2002. *The memory bible*. New York: Hyperion.

Sprenger, M. 2005. *How to teach so students remember.* Alexandria, Virginia: Association for Supervision and Curriculum Development.

Sprenger, M. 2007. *Memory 101 for educators*. Corwin Press.

Starko, A. 2004. *Creativity in the classroom*. Mahwah, NJ: Lawrence Erlbaum.

Sternberg, R. J., and Williams, W. M. 1996. *How to develop student creativity*. Alexandria, VA: Association for Supervision and Curriculum Development.

Stevick, E. W. 1996. *Memory, meaning and method: second edition*. Boston: Newbury House.

Stevick, E. W. 1998. *Working with teaching methods*. Boston, MA: Heinle.

Stoller, F. L. 2007. *Graphic organizers: Versatile tools for promoting language and content learning.* Paper presented at 16ᵗʰ International Symposium and Book Fair on English Teaching, Ming Chuan University, Taiwan.

Thiagarajan, S. and Thiagarajan, R. 2003. *Design your own games and activities.* San Francisco, CA: Jossey-Bass/Pfeiffer.

Treffinger, D. J. 2000. *Practice problems for creative problem solving.* Waco, TX: Prufrock Press.

Von Oech, R. 2008. *A whack on the side of the head.* New York: Business Plus.

Von Oech, R. 1986. *A kick in the seat of the pants.* New York: Harper.

Willis, D. and Willis, J. 2007. *Doing task-based teaching.* Oxford University Press.

RECOMMENDED WEBSITES

Memory

Build Your Memory
http://www.buildyourmemory.com/

Mind Tools - Memory Improvement Techniques
http://www.mindtools.com/memory.html

Exploratorium - The Memory Exhibition
http://www.exploratorium.edu/memory/index.html

Science Museum - Your Brain - Memory
http://www.sciencemuseum.org.uk/on-line/brain/260.asp

Neuroscience for Kids - Memory Experiments
http://faculty.washington.edu/chudler/chmemory.html

The Memory Experience – BBC
http://www.bbc.co.uk/sn/tvradio/programmes/memory/

Creativity

Idea Generation Techniques – Jack Martin Leith
http://www.jackmartinleith.com/idea-generation-methods/index.
html

Creativity Web
http://members.optusnet.com.au/~charles57/Creative/

Creative Thinking – Michael Michalko's Home Page
http://www.creativethinking.net/

Mycoted
http://www.mycoted.com/Main_Page

Gocreate.com
http://gocreate.com/index.htm

23 Creativity Techniques - Alfred S. Alschuler
http://www2.gsu.edu/~dscthw/x130/CREATIVE/Techniques.html

Mind Tools - Creativity Tools, Solutions, and Problem Solving
Techniques
http://www.mindtools.com/pages/main/newMN_CT.htm

Robert Harris - Creative Thinking Techniques
http://www.virtualsalt.com/crebook2.htm

Creatingminds.org – Tools for creating ideas
http://www.creatingminds.org/tools/tool_ideation.htm

Dr. Leslie Wilson – Creativity Index
http://www.uwsp.edu/education/lwilson/creativ/index.htm

Critical Thinking

The Critical Thinking Community
http://www.criticalthinking.org/

Mission: Critical
http://www.sjsu.edu/depts/itl/graphics/main.html

Critical Thinking Web
http://philosophy.hku.hk/think/

The Nizkor Project – Fallacies
http://www.nizkor.org/features/fallacies/

Fallacy Files
http://www.fallacyfiles.org/

The Logical Fallacies
http://www.onegoodmove.org/fallacy/toc.htm

Graphic Organizers

Using Graphic Organizers
http://www.carla.umn.edu/cobaltt/modules/strategies/gorganizers/index.html

The Graphic Organizer
http://www.graphic.org/goindex.html

Schools of California Online Resources for Education - Graphic Organizers
http://www.sdcoe.k12.ca.us/SCORE/actbank/torganiz.htm

Graphic Organizers - Guidelines
http://www.wm.edu/ttac/articles/learning/graphic.html

Graphic Organizers
http://www.ncrel.org/sdrs/areas/issues/students/learning/lr1grorg.htm

Graphic Organizers as Thinking Technology
http://www.fno.org/oct97/picture.html

Graphic Organizers
http://www.squires.fayette.k12.ky.us/library/research/problem6.htm

ABOUT THE AUTHOR

Hall Houston teaches undergraduate students at Kainan University, a private university in Taoyuan County, Taiwan. His practical articles on language teaching have appeared in *It's for Teachers, One Stop English, Humanising Language Teaching, Developing Teachers, English Teaching Professional, Modern English Teacher, ESL Magazine, The Internet TESL Journal*, and *Language Magazine*. His first book, *The Creative Classroom*, was published in 2007 by Lynx Publishing. His professional interests include task-based teaching and learning, discourse analysis, group dynamics, creativity and critical thinking.

INDEX

Getting to know each other

Guessing

Review

Role play

Student feedback

Warmers

Made in the USA
Charleston, SC
22 January 2011